The MYSTERY FANcier

**Volume 1   Number 5
September 1977**

THE MYSTERY FANCIER

Volume 1 Number 5
September 1977

TABLE OF CONTENTS

MYSTERIOUSLY SPEAKING 1
Piercing the Closed Circle: The Technique of Point of
   View in Works by P.D. James, by Jane S. Bakerman . . 3
Fear and Loathing With the Lone Wolf, by George Kelley. . 17
The Avon Classic Crime Collection, by Jeff Meyerson . . . 19
The Nero Wolfe Saga, Part III, by Guy M. Townsend 21
MYSTERY*FILE: Short Reviews by Steve Lewis: Forrest, *The Wizard of Death*; Maling, *Schroeder's Game*; Woods, *The Law's Delay*; Burns, *The Farnsworth Score*; Ferris, *High Places*; Masterson, *Hunter of the Blood*; Jahn, *The Quark Maneuver*; Hall, *Exit Sherlock Holmes*; Egan, *The Blind Search*; Pronzini, *Blowback*; Aarons, *Assignment Afghan Dragon*; Martin, *The Deal of the Century*; Patterson, *The Thomas Berryman Number*; Washburn, *The Armageddon Game*; Linzee, *Death in Connecticut*; Garfield, *Recoil*; Brown, *The Stripper*; MacKenzie, *Death Is a Friend*; Bailey, *The Red Castle Mystery*; Crane, *The Cinnamon Murder*; York, *The Fascinator*; Knox, *Rally to Kill*; Coxe, *The Glass Triangle*. 29
VERDICTS (More Reviews): Mcdonald, *Fletch and Confess*, *Fletch* (Meyerson); Brett, *So Much Blood* (Townsend); Morrison, *Best Martin Hewitt Detective Stories* (Townsend); Rinehart, *The Circular Staircase* (Wooster); Vidal, *Matters of Fact & Fiction: Essays 1973-1976* (Kelley); McBain, *Even the Wicked* (Broset); McBain, *Where There's Smoke* (Broset); Moore, *The Terminal Connection* (Broset); Curtis, *The Savage Women*, Andrews, *Body Rub*, Conaway, *The Deadly Spring* (Kabatchnik); Anderson, *The Affair of the Blood-Stained Egg Cosy* (Meyerson); Laumer, *Pat Chance* (Lansdale); Simenon, *Maigret and the Black Sheep*, Freeling, *The Bugles Blowing* (Nevins); Ball, *The Eyes of Buddha* (Nevins); Charteris, *The Saint in New York* (Meyerson); Holding, *The Blank Wall* (Bakerman); Gruber, *The French Key Mystery* (Meyerson); Blanc, *The Green Stone* (Williams); Spewack, *Murder in the Gilded Cage* (Shibuk); Miller, *Guilty Bystander* (Meyerson); Talbot, *Rim of the Pit* (Meyerson); Hamilton, *Murderer's Row* (Meyerson); Gardner, *TCOT Queenly Contestant* (Nevins); Gardner, *TCOT Careless Cupid* (Nevins); Gardner, *TCOT Fabulous Fake* (Nevins); Hall, *Exit Sherlock Holmes* (Townsend)... . 37
THE DOCUMENTS IN THE CASE (Letters): Juri; Sorrell; Lansdale; Wooster; Meyerson; Briney; Williams; Kelley; Pross; Cole. 53

Subscription rates: $7.50 per year (6 issues) US; $9.00 overseas; single issue price $1.50. ISSN: 0146-3160.
The MYSTERY FANcier is edited and published by Guy M. Townsend, 1256 Pidgeon Perch Lane, Memphis, TN 38116 USA.
Deadline for November issue: 1 October 1977.

Copyright © 1977 by Guy M. Townsend
All rights reserved for contributors.

MYSTERIOUSLY SPEAKING...

Several of this issue's letter writers expressed what I suspect most of you were thinking--that the smaller, fuzzier type of the new format is made even more difficult to read by being printed on colored paper. So I have experimented and I *think* I can print this on white mimeo paper without too much of a show-through problem. At any rate I'm going to try.

Most of the response to the format change has been either favorable or at least tolerant, the most notable exception being Martin Wooster. (But then Martin never approves of anything.)

The proposed increase in first class postal rates will eat up the last of the savings I made by going to the smaller size, but I don't foresee having to raise subscription rates for volume two. In fact, overseas rates will be lowered somewhat for subscriptions sent via surface mail, and air mail subs will be available for $12.00 or $13.00 (it costs better than $1.00 per issue to airmail TMF to Europe).

I continue to be desperate for cover art. I cannot believe that TMF has no artistically inclined subscribers, and I'm beginning to get a bit miffed at you folks for not sharing your gifts with the rest of us.

WARNING ::: In her otherwise admirable article on P.D. James, Jane Bakerman reveals the identities of a number of James's murderers, so readers planning to sample James in the near future are advised to save Jane's article for a later, rainy day.

Another warning, of sorts. Steve gives Hall's *Exit Sherlock Holmes* a pretty favorable review in this issue's "Mystery*File". My own reaction to the book was so different that, when I found myself with a page and a half to fill to round this issue out to an even sixty pages, I decided to inflict upon you an opinionated review of the same book, which I had done a while back for the local rag. I do not apologize for the opinions--only for the style; I am more inclined to preach to the general reader than I am to the mystery fancier.

I have at last arrived at that much wished for state of having more material than I can use in the present issue. On hand, already typed up and ready for reduction, is "Raymond Chandler on Film: An Annotated Checklist", the article Peter Pross mentions in his letter in this issue's "Documents in the Case". When I began to put this issue together I wasn't sure how much I had on hand, though it seemed to be more than enough. I typed all the articles first (except the Saga), then I did the letters and finally the reviews. Counting up, I saw that I would have to cut somewhere if I was to continue the Saga uninterrupted (which I am determined to do), so it was eliminate an article or some reviews. In retrospect I think it would have been better to hold off on some reviews, since there are twenty-four pages of them, but my reasoning at the time was that the reviews of new material really needed to be aired as soon as possible, so

I did not want to cut them, and there were so few reviews of older material that I didn't want to cut them either. Besides, it is easier to carry a single article over to the next issue than it is to carry over a handful of reviews, particularly when there is likely to be an abundance of reviews for the next issue anyway.

What I would like to see in TMF is a roughly 2:1:1 ratio: thirty pages of articles, fifteen of reviews and fifteen of letters. In the present issue there are twenty-eight pages of articles, twenty-four of reviews and only eight pages of letters. Reviews are the easiest things to do, which is why we have so many of them, and they certainly are useful. But they are nowhere near as interesting (or as much fun) either to read or to write as a good meaty article or letter of comment. So let's have more articles and letters, fellow fanciers. Okay?

By the way, if there are those among you who disagree with the 2:1:1 ratio for TMF, please speak out and state your preferences. I am neither humble nor particularly obedient, but I am your servant, after a fashion, and I aim to please.

Jeff Meyerson has graciously offered to do the index of books reviewed in volume one of TMF. It will appear in 2:1 and will no doubt be of great use to everyone; I know that I often have a hell of a time finding a review that I have read in these pages.

Lastly, since I have some space left on this page, a few words about the title of this publication. When, after a surprisingly difficult time of cudgeling my brain for decent names which sounded okay and weren't too cute ("The Mystery Monger" was the only other thing I could come up with, but it would have been a nonsense title for this publication), I decided to call this "The Mystery Fancier", I thought I would indulge myself and emphasize the "mystery fan" in "The Mystery Fancier" by capitalizing the title thusly: The MYSTERY FANcier. This has turned out to be a real can of worms; I would not have thought it possible for so many variants to emerge, the most common being The Mystery FANcier which, among other things, is asymmetrical. Indeed, I fear it may remain The Mystery FANcier forever, to my (and Poirot's) eternal discomfort. So I'm giving up. Capitalize it however you please--every other letter if you like. As for me, I'm going to swear off fancy-title creating for life.

PRE 1961 PAPERBACKS FOR SALE. Pocket Books, Dells, Popular Library, Signet, Bantam and many others for sale at low prices (most $1 or less). List is made up of mostly mysteries with many Gardner Pocket Books. Fill up those gaps in your collections CHEAPLY. List 25¢.
S. D. Owen, P.O. Box 343, Moraga, CA 94556.

PIERCING THE CLOSED CIRCLE:
The Technique of Point of View
in Works by P.D. James
By Jane S. Bakerman

I

One of the most important trends in the development of the mystery-detective story is the growing attention being paid to genuine and valid motivation. And one of the best current practitioners of the craft who is very much *in* that trend is P.D. James (Phyllis White) whose first six novels—*Cover Her Face* (London: Faber and Faber, 1962); *A Mind to Murder* (New York: Charles Scribner's Sons, 1963); *Unnatural Causes* (New York: Popular Library, 1967); *Shroud for a Nightingale* (London: Sphere Books Limited, 1973); *An Unsuitable Job for a Woman* (New York: Charles Scribner's Sons, 1972); and *The Black Tower* (New York: Charles Scribner's Sons, 1975)—are not only exciting, well plotted mysteries, but also fascinating studies in human psychology.

James achieves a very special (but never burdensome) psychological intensity primarily through her use of the closed society, penetrated by an outsider—or a set of outsiders—and by her clever employment of the multiple point of view. The effort is entirely conscious on her part, for she sees these devices as enriching to the works as well as being practical. For the mystery-detective student or fan, an examination of these methods is illuminating and interesting.

II

Patterns of social organization and their relationships to human motivation are intriguing to the author, and she has spoken of that interest:
> I think that the interaction of human beings in a closed society is absolutely fascinating: the power struggles, the attempt to establish and retain one's own identity, the way in which people group defensive or offensive alliances, particularly against strangers. And I think, too, that there's a certain dramatic element in the detective coming *into* this society, penetrating it, seeing it with fresh eyes—and the whole society react to him. Of course, it's also convenient in that if you have a closed society, then you have a closed circle of suspects.[1]

The closed social circle is usually formed, in a James book, through a familial or professional relationship, though once the professional is re-enforced by locale, and once through physical disability. The members are not usually drawn together by love—save in the case of the family—but rather by self-interest, circumstance, or the need to protect professional reputations.

The major penetrator is always the detective—usually, James' continuing character Adam Dalgliesh, but once Cordelia Gray (*An Unsuitable Job for a Woman*), a private detective. In at least one instance, the victim, Sally Jupp (*Cover Her Face*), is also very clearly a penetrator, but that circumstance is unusual. Dalgliesh is always aware of himself as penetrator, interloper, for this poet-policeman is not only tough but also sensitive. He is consistently mindful of the fact that he *both* sets things to rights by finding and removing the murderer *and* leaves the closed society forever altered. This awareness that not only the disruptive but the healing force as well impose change upon the closed society lends a good measure of tension and intensity.

In all instances, the members of the closed society, while suspicious of one another, are tentative or even hostile toward the detectives. The members want the crimes to be solved, of course, but they are tense and resentful about the fact that solution will surely identify one of their own number as the murderer. Their common identity seems to overshadow even fear of the murderer and a kind of awareness that he or she is one type of penetrator who also wears the guise of membership. Further, since James' characters may not always be likeable but are always bright, they are all clever enough to know that the investigator must penetrate *them*—explore their various personalities and motives as well as the corporate personality and aims of the group—and they resent and resist that process.

This level of tension has been well characterized by James herself:

> I want people to be interested in my characters, and therefore, I think it's advisable, probably sensible, to see things through their eyes. And I think it's quite effective for the reader to get to know them and then for the detective to come in. It also can be quite intriguing because the reader will often feel that he knows them better than the detective. I mean, I know that in detective fiction, you must never *hide* anything from your reader, but I think it's equally intriguing to hide things from your detective: the detective will come in and see someone, but that's not quite how *we* see it; he's not quite *right* about it.[2]

To achieve this tension, then, James must usually forego using only the detective himself to provide point of view (though she does so very beautifully in *An Unsuitable Job for a Woman*). But she does not find that limitation hampering:

> Well, I think greater richness and complexity are achieved by this ability to see certain incidents, certain scenes of the novel, through another's eyes—I think it's very difficult if everything is seen through the detective's eyes—so much, then, can't be described.[3]

Nor does she find the first person point of view terribly attractive:

> I think the first person is often a very tempting and possibly very satisfactory form; it's an

egotistical form, but at least it's direct; it encourages the writer to be himself and to describe what he has seen . . . but certainly it can lead, I think, to a certain flatness and lack of interest.[4]

There's far more richness in a novel where one is able to enter into different human beings and particularly to see the *same* event through their different eyes. A small example of that is in *A Mind to Murder*, when the body is discovered, and because it's a nervous reaction that he has, the consulting psychiatrist, Dr. Steiner, has to turn away because he finds he's giggling. And it's purely nothing he can control. And to the other person there, he seems to be weeping, and to her, it's extraordinary that he should be so distressed over the death of someone he didn't in fact like. I think this is useful; it adds psychological tone.[5]

The result, then, of this elimination of the first person point of view is the use of multiple points of view. There is, really, no omniscient voice in the James novel, but instead, the reader is closely involved by identifying with or reacting against a number of characters all treated in the third person, who provide--or conceal--various insights. Since the reader also tends to identify with Dalgliesh because he is an attractive and powerful figure, the level of involvement is unusual. The reader is both member of the closed circle, through his interest in and analysis of the points of view of the members, *and* is at one with the penetrator, the detective, as he or she unravels the mystery.

One of the difficult and sometimes awkward scenes traditional to the mystery novel is the unraveling, the explanation by the detective of his process of deduction. Certainly James employs these scenes, though she, like some other good writers, varies them a bit--once, she uses a tape recorded by the killer (*Unnatural Causes*), for instance, once a combination of confrontation between killer and detective and a letter (*Shroud for a Nightingale*), as well as the standard, "Meet me in the library at eight, and I'll explain all" (*Cover Her Face*). But the James books avoid the tedium and the arrogance sometimes apparent in this type of scene--the reason is primarily that multiple point of view.

By the time the explanation occurs, the reader knows all the characters very well, and the motivations, while never boringly obvious, ring true and remain intriguing. Further, since the reader has been exploring and evaluating the minds of almost all the characters, his "Ah, yes; *that's it!*" response is always gratifying, never belittling to his own puzzle-solving ability. All the clues have been given fairly, and he is able to piece together the rationale of and behind the puzzle. That is, since James murders are rarely done by someone so hateful that there are almost too many suspects, the problem must be resolved by the revelation of genuine, powerful motivations. It always is so resolved. Human needs and impulses are thoroughly explored and examined; human capacity for evil is surveyed, and the chaotic world is set aright, but forever changed and altered. As in life.

Thus, readers become both members of the society and

its penetrators; they identify with a range of characters and explore with them a variety of human motives and intentions. The pattern is always present, always neat, but never pat nor formulaic, for the device is varied nicely in each novel.

III

James' first novel, *Cover Her Face*, shares a setting common to the English detective story. The place is Martingale, a country house, identified as near Chadfleet and Nessingford. The core of the closed society (one closed society within another, a pattern common in these books) is the Maxie family: Eleanor, the mother, is devoting herself to nursing her fatally ill husband and to striving to make ends meet in their much reduced circumstances. Her divorced daughter, Deborah Maxie Riscoe, assists Mrs. Maxie in these efforts, both women serving not only the invalid Simon Maxie but also the son, Stephen, whose birthright must be preserved and whose medical training must not be interrupted. The outer cluster of the closed society is formed by local friends, lovers, and acquaintances whose presence lends color, plot complication, and depth.

Initially, this society is penetrated by the junior housemaid, Sally Jupp, an unwed mother whose personality is steadily revealed as being selfish and destructive. Sally represents not only the stranger within the gates but also the intrusion of another class and other social standards. She manages to wound almost everyone with whom she associates, but it is not until Sally's engagement to Stephen Maxie is flaunted before the family and their friends--all her benefactors--that the murder takes place. Sally, like most of the James victims, has violated a central rule of the closed society; in this case, responsible social behavior. The murder, of course, introduces Dalgliesh, the ultimate penetrator.

James dramatizes the intrusion directly:

> The Maxies, Felix Hearne and Catherine Bowers stood together at the open graveside with Miss Liddell and a handful of girls from St. Mary's bunched behind them. Opposite them stood Dalgliesh and Martin [his aide]. Police and suspects faced each other across the open grave. (p. 150)

Because the murderer is surely one of the circle, there is no gladness, no relief when the police arrive to impose order; and this pattern is complicated by the fact that the Inspector is regarded as an interloper by the local constabulary also:

> The local superintendent was waiting in the hall. They knew each other slightly as was to be expected with two men both eminent in the same job, but neither had ever wished for a closer acquaintanceship. It was not an easy moment. (p. 61)[6]

There are four main points of view (besides that of Dalgliesh) employed in *Cover Her Face*, first those of Deborah Maxie Riscoe, Catherine Bowers, and Felix Hearne. Employing these characters is effective because the reader shares their special, compelling interests. Deborah is at a turning point in her life, and she is also attracted to Dalgliesh. Catherine matures in the course of the novel by being forced to come to a true understanding of Stephen Maxie, whom she loves. Felix, terrified of the police because of his experiences with the Gestapo, must not only face his fear but also face the end of his term as Deborah's lover.

But the most fascinating point of view used extensively is that of Eleanor Maxie, a strong, admirable woman who is also the murderer. Despite the fact that James has said the point of view of the murderer cannot be employed because after the crime, "the guilty person would have the murder in his mind the whole time,"[7] she does so here. This usage raises the question of fairness to the reader, and, generally speaking, James is fair.[8] It's a remarkable juggling act.

An examination of some of these key passages shows both the general fairness to the reader and the subtle clues the Eleanor Maxie point of view provides in retrospect. Twice, for instance, James uses Eleanor's perceptions to explore the night of the murder:

> [She] kept her vigil on the day bed in his [her sick husband's] dressing-room and heard the hours strike while the luminous hand on the clock beside her bed jerked forward towards the inevitable day. She lived through the scene in the drawing-room so many times that there now seemed no second of it which was not remembered with clarity, no nuance of voice or emotion which was lost. (p. 54)

The scene in the drawing room, of course, triggered the murder.

The second moment dramatizes, when the truth is known, the murderer's isolation and the terror of coming events:

> At six o'clock she got up and put on her dressing-gown, then she filled and plugged in the electric kettle for her morning tea. The day with its problems had come at last.
>
> It was a relief to her when there was a knock on the door. . . . Mrs. Maxie had a moment of acute fear that Catherine had come to talk, that the affairs of the previous evening would have to be discussed, assessed, deprecated and re-lived. She had spent most of the night making plans that she could not share nor would wish to share with Catherine. But she found herself unaccountably glad to see another human being. (pp. 55-56)

Within moments, James reminds the reader, as he realizes after the unraveling, that sympathy for Eleanor Maxie must be laced with awareness (and condemnation) of her wrongdoing. Mrs. Maxie shares that awareness:

> Mrs. Maxie replaced her cup in its saucer and noticed with clinical detachment and a kind of wonder that her hand was not shaking. The imminence of evil took hold and she had to pause for a second before she could trust her voice. But when the words came, neither Catherine nor Martha seemed aware of any change in her. (p. 56)

In a stroke, the author invokes evil and Mrs. Maxie becomes identified, as is later realized, as the veiled penetrator; she *has* changed; a life devoted to nurturing has become a life caught up in destruction. The juggling act is difficult, but it is done very well, indeed, particularly for a first novel. The reader accepts the motivation--the wild effort to protect a dying husband's peace and son's threatened future--inexcusable, but understandable.

An Unsuitable Job for a Woman is, perhaps, James' best novel to date; certainly it has been widely praised. This book introduces one of the author's most well realized and entrancing characters, Cordelia Gray, a strong, independent, sensitive and insightful young woman who is also an apprentice private detective. Upon the suicide of her senior partner, Cordelia inherits their agency and almost immediately thereafter gets her first real case; she is hired to investigate the death of a young former student. Thus, though the book begins and ends in London (another James circle; there are loads of them), the major action takes place in Cambridge.

There are two closed societies which Cordelia must penetrate; both clearly perceived her as an interloper, although the head of the first, Sir Ronald Callender, has employed her to investigate his son's death. Callender heads a scientific research team, and their intense bonds are mainly professional though sometimes personal, for two team members love Callender--Elizabeth Leaming, his secretary, and Chris Lunn, his technician, whom Callender has rescued from the streets . . . again the nucleus within the slightly larger closed circle.

The second is particularly fascinating and is composed of students who were loyal friends to the victim, Mark Callender. Cordelia is strongly attracted to these young people and they to her, although the relationship, of course, is complicated. Cordelia, who has no family and has just lost her only friend, must constantly guard against the attractiveness of the group--Hugh and Sophie Trilling, Isabelle deLasterie, and Davie Stevens. Her strong sense of the integrity of her work, a deep commitment to the victim, and her well realized sense of self serve to provide the counterbalance. As usual, James is careful to dramatise all this tension. She does so by sharing Cordelia's thought processes as she weighs their behavior and their motivation:

> They had some guilty knowledge; that had been obvious. Why else had they reacted so strongly to her arrival? They wanted the facts of Mark Callender's death to be left undisturbed. They would try to persuade, cajole, even to shame her into abandoning the case. Would they, she wondered, also threaten? But why? The most likely theory was that they were shielding someone. But again, why? Murder wasn't a matter of climbing late into college, a venial infringement of rules which a friend would automatically condone and conceal. Mark Callender had been their friend; to two of them he might have been more than a friend. Someone whom he knew and trusted had pulled a strap tight round his neck, had watched and listened to his agonizing choking, had strung his body on a hook like the carcass of an animal. How could one reconcile that appalling knowledge with Davie Stevens' slightly amused and rueful glance at Sophie, with Hugo's cynical calm,

with Sophie's friendly and interested eyes? If they were conspirators, then they were monsters. (p. 67)

The immediacy is intense, and the involvement of the reader is very great indeed, for here, James also provides a psychological study of Cordelia which is more detailed and more accessible than the more frequent but more limited studies of Dalgliesh himself.

Eventually, Cordelia does penetrate all the circles and solve the crime. Immediately after doing so, she becomes a criminal herself, for the orignial murderer is killed in vengeance and retribution. Judging this act to be, in a sense, just, Cordelia helps the second murderer to conceal the crime. Now, Cordelia has uncovered all the secrets; unwillingly she is a member of both closed societies, but also forever barred from them, for she knows too much. Because she knows too much, they are uneasy about her power—and Dalgliesh must attempt to break her defenses. He does not; and the reason for his failure is one of James' cleverest manipulations of point of view.

Cordelia's partner, Bernie Pryde, had once been Dalgliesh's subordinate, but had been dismissed because he wasn't, really, very able. All his tattered life, however, Bernie had revered the Superintendent, and in training Cordelia, Bernie had constantly and accurately quoted Dalgliesh to her. More able than her teacher, Cordelia, whose fondness for Bernie causes her to hate this authority figure from his past, nevertheless faithfully puts Dalgliesh's precepts to work. Over and over again in the book, we get secondhand Dalgliesh; despite the fact that she despises him, Cordelia must come to realize that "the Super" knows what he is doing, and she proves his methods to be good. The result is ironic and gently humorous, a nice offset to the rather particular horror of the crime under investigation here.

Importantly, it is Dalgliesh dogma that triggers her close identification with the victim, Mark Callender:
> What was it that the supercilious, sapient, super-human Super had taught? "Get to know the dead person. Nothing about him is too trivial, too unimportant. Dead men can talk. They can lead you directly to their murderer." (p. 25)

And, indeed, Mark so does.

The tone of these memories is consistent while Cordelia is working on the original crime:
> She remembered another reported pearl of the Superintendent's wisdom: "Detection requires a patient persistence which amounts to obstinacy." She thought of him as she dialled the first number. What an intolerably demanding and irritating boss he must have been! But he was almost certainly old now—forty-five at least. He had probably eased up a bit by now. (p. 112)

But that tone, along with her perception of Dalgliesh, alters when she gets caught up in the second crime. She uses, for instance, his experience to manage to disguise the second murder as suicide, remembering hearing Barnie say:
> "That's the little mistake Mrs. Clandon made and it nearly hanged her. She shot her husband behind the right ear with his service revolver and

then tried to fake a suicide. But she pressed the
wrong finger on the trigger. If he'd really shot
himself behind the right ear he'd have pressed the
trigger with his thumb and held the revolver with
his palm round the back of the butt. I remember
that case well. It was the first murder I worked on
with the Super--Inspector Dalgliesh, as he was then."
(p. 148)

Again, when she must stand as witness at the inquest
for this crime, when her secondhand technique will be strictly tested, it's Dalgliesh-as-echo who pulls her through:

> She remembered a piece of Dalgliesh dogma, reported by Bernie, which had seemed to her at the
> time more appropriate advice for a criminal [which
> she has now become] than a detective. "Never tell
> an unnecessary lie; the truth has great authority.
> The cleverest murders have been caught, not because
> they told the essential lie, but because they continued to lie about unimportant detail when the
> truth could have done them no harm." (p. 160)

Cordelia's most stringent test comes when Dalgliesh
(presumably using those very methods the reader has watched
Cordelia test) solves the second murder to his intellectual
satisfaction but has no proof; Cordelia is summoned for an
interview:

> Bernie had been right. She recalled his advice;
> the Superintendent's advice; this time she could almost hear it spoken in his deep, slightly husky
> voice: "If you're tempted to crime, stick to your
> original statement. There's nothing that impresses
> the jury more than consistency. I've seen the most
> unlikely defence succeed simply because the accused
> stuck to his story. After all, it's only someone
> else's word against yours; with a competent counsel,
> that's half-way to a reasonable doubt." (p. 180)

Here, the competent counsel is Dalgliesh-Pryde, and
though the policeman knows he's right he can prove nothing.
His own precepts make him, for once, unable to penetrate,
and James' most intriguing experiment with multiple point of
view (Gray-Pryde-Dalgliesh, a club sandwich point of view)
ends a resounding success. Sharing Cordelia's reasoning,
the reader comes to know not only her but Bernie and the policeman as well as all the members of the closed circles;
her efforts to think as they do provide multiplicity in a
special way and dramatize the motivations with startling effectiveness.

Cordelia emerges mature, her integrity intact, but a
criminal of sorts. Crime, no matter how well intended, is
never excused in a James novel, and Cordelia pays a price.
Unwillingly, Cordelia Gray and Adam Dalgliesh have formed,
through Bernie, the final closed circle in this intricate
plot; each has come to recognize the other as able, attractive and worthy. Yet the circle must remain a cold one;
real friendship--or even love--cannot be pursued, for the
potentially rewarding relationship is really blocked by Cordelia's success as a student and by Dalgliesh's success as
a secondhand teacher.

IV

The other four in this group of novels—*A Mind to Murder, Unnatural Causes, Shroud for a Nightingale,* and *The Black Tower*—follow more closely the standard James pattern; as always the closed circles are effectively present, and the multiple point of view is handled well but more directly.

In *A Mind to Murder*, set in London, the larger closed circle is the Steen Clinic for psychological and psychiatric outpatient care; and again, there are circles within circles. Some of the employees are lovers and former lovers; two are related, and the expectable professional cliques have been formed. The murdered woman is Enid Bolam, the chief administrative officer, revealed to be stuffy but not, perhaps, hateful. Dalgliesh is cleverly led astray in this investigation, and the reasons are well documented by the author:

> The clinic staff, excluded from these [detection] activities and congregated in the front ground-floor consulting-room . . . felt that their familiar ground had been taken over by strangers and that they were caught up in the inexorable machinery of justice and being ground forward to God knew what embarrassments and disasters. (p. 32)

one of the clearest statements of the closed-circle-attitude in the canon. Gradually, through the points of view of such characters as Paul Steiner, Mrs. Shorthouse (one of James' most charming characterizations), and Fredrica Saxon, the complex motivations of these bright but all-too-human people emerge.

One set of motivations, however, do reveal a special James twist, for in just one passage (pp. 121-122), the reader enters the mind of the perpetrator post-crime. But this passage is fair to the reader, and when reconsidered at the end of the story, deepens it touchingly. The murderer, Marion Bolam, is responsible for the care of her invalid mother; money is short, and the mother, despite her efforts not to do so, depends entirely on Marion for emotional sustenance as well as for economic support. The passage is nicely done. Once sensitized to what is going on, the reader is able to recognize the intense effort Marion is making not to think of the details of this day on which she has done murder and her dread that she will be unable to tolerate the usual questions about the minute workings of her day. Again, the pattern works, and *A Mind to Murder* is a satisfying book.

Unnatural Causes gives short shrift to writers who forget human values! This book employs a frame device: Dalgliesh has again met Deborah Maxie Riscoe in *A Mind to Murder*, and here he comes away to his aunt's home in a writers' colony, Monksmere Head on the Suffolk Coast, to decide if he will marry her. *Causes'* larger closed circle is the group of writers—Jane Dalgliesh, Oliver Latham, Justin Bryce, Celia Calthrop, Maurice Seton, and R. B. Sinclair. The smaller, inner circles are formed by their social, professional and familial alliances (this is the only story to date in which we observe Dalgliesh in a close, family association, and it's a good one), and there is one tangential circle, a grim part of the London underworld.

Here is provided the best example of the circle's coming to accept the fact that the penetrator *must* function; they are beginning to face reality:

> By half-past eight they had all arrived. No one had troubled to fetch Sylvia Kedge, but apart from her the little company of five nights earlier was met again. And Dalgliesh was struck by the difference in them. Analysing it, he realized that they looked ten years older. Five nights ago they had been only mildly concerned and a little intrigued by Seton's disappearance. Now they were anxious and shaken, possessed by images of blood and death from which they had little hope of shaking free. Behind the assumptions of ease, the rather desperate attempts at normality, he could smell fear.
>
> Maurice Seton had died in London and it was still theoretically possible to believe that he had died naturally or that someone in London was responsible for his murder if not for the mutilation of his body. But Digby's death was on home ground and no one could pretend that there had been anything natural about it. (pp. 208-209)

The colony clearly perceived Dalgliesh as an alien penetrator, a sort of poet-gone-wrong, and here, as in *Cover Her Face*, the vacationing policeman must juggle protocol, for the local officer, Inspector Reckless, is really in charge.

The multiple point of view represents one of James' most interesting portraits, Celia Calthrop, not likeable at first glance, but as the reader shares her mind, he learns not only her easily observed weaknesses but also her strengths. Here, too, is the James twist, for in one short chapter (pp. 140-143) the mind of a murderer, Sylvia Kedge, is entered after the crime. No rules are violated. At first reading, Sylvia's thoughts can be attributed to her status in life and in the colony, her loneliness, and her fear of a coming, terrible storm. It is only after the book is finished that the passage falls into place on another level, a splendid symbol of her psychological torment. But here, as in *A Mind to Murder*, the twist is handled much more sparely than in *Cover Her Face*. Like this device, the book is effective.

The nursing school of the John Carpendar Hospital near the Sussex-Hampshire border, Nightingale House, is the setting for *Shroud for a Nightingale*. Obviously, the student nurses, their teachers, and the hospital staff provide the basic closed circle, within which friendships and love affairs offer smaller closed societies. Again, a frame is employed, for the story begins and ends in the mind of Miss Muriel Beale, Inspector of Nurse Training Schools of the General Nursing Council. Miss Beale provides us with a detached point of view, lots of common sense, and, importantly, because of her job, she, like Dalgliesh, is clearly a penetrator. This device serves not only as a handy plotting tool but also as a symbol of the larger world's steady infringement upon the closed society.

A murderer, Mary Taylor, is James' most stunning example of the secret, masked penetrator, and again, the multiple point of view provides us with several memorable characterizations, especially Morag Smith and Sister Mavis Gearing, a member of the teaching staff and another of James' portraits of a woman not to be dismissed too lightly. Through the minds and voices of these and other characters, personalities and motivations are deftly drawn.

It is important to note that this book explores most closely the harsher effects of the closed society; it is *not* always a haven, and James knows it:

> She had given him a depressing glimpse into the stultifying lack of privacy, and of the small pettinesses and subterfuges with which people living in unwelcome proximity try to preserve their own privacy or invade that of others. The thought of . . . two adult lovers creeping furtively down a back staircase to avoid detection was grotesque and humiliating. . . . Small wonder that Nightingale House bred its own brand of neurosis, that Sister Gearing found it necessary to justify a walk with her lover in the grounds . . . with unconvincing twaddle about the need to discuss hospital business. He found it all profoundly depressing and he wasn't sorry when it was time to let her go. (p. 124)

Even the inner circles, drawn by love, are not without their limitations and pressures; Dalgliesh speaks:

> And Brumfett had stuck to you ever since. When you came here she followed. The impulse to confide, the need to have at least one friend who knew all about you, put you in her power. Brumfett, the protector, adviser, confidante. Theatres with Brumfett; morning golf with Brumfett; holidays with Brumfett; country drives with Brumfett; early morning tea and last night drinks with Brumfett. Her devotion must have been real enough. After all, she was willing to kill for you. But it was blackmail all the same. A more orthodox blackmailer, merely demanding a regular tax-free income, would have been infinitely preferable to Brumfett's intolerable devotion. (p. 284)

As always in the James books, the solutions to the murders change the closed circle forever—as the members know from the start and tend to resist. But in *Shroud*, though people are dead, able professionals forever out of service, friendships violated and lovers separated, the final changes are redemptive, and the story ends on a note of hope, symbolized by the destruction of Nightingale House to make way for a new school. *Shroud for a Nightingale* is a splendid book, valid in its construction and in its human values.

The Black Tower, however, is a grim book, and though the reader is convinced that the sheltering circle *had* to change, he is not terribly hopeful at the end. *Tower* is set on the Purbeck coast at Toynton Grange, "a private home for the young disabled." (p. 13) The major circle is composed of the patients and the staff, the inner closed societies, again, by their friends, lovers, and families. Dalgliesh is drawn here by the call of an old friend, Father Baddeley, and by his own need for a place to recover from a serious illness. That illness has triggered an impulse to retire from the force, and his struggle with that temptation forms the frame for the book, a history which provides the most intimate examination of the detective's own personality and values.

Here, much of the time we share Dalgliesh's point of view, but the visits into the minds of some of the other characters, particularly Grace Willison and Ursula Hollis, provide not only useful, necessary background and clues, but also some remarkably effective insights into the world and the psychology of the hopelessly ill. Frequently their innocence overlapped with Dalgliesh's slightly more cynical vision is the key to the reader's needed insights into the motivation of two special benefactors to the patients. Wilfred Anstey, who runs the home, is a devout man, supposedly motivated by only the most noble impulses. He is contrasted brilliantly with the worldly Julius Court, whose generous response to the needs of the patients is initially puzzling, but, in the end, very clear indeed.

Julius Court is the murderer in *Tower*, and James' use of him as participant during the basic action is very clever. The final unraveling takes place in a long, active, danger-filled scene between him and Dalgliesh, probably the most melodramatic in the whole series of books . . . but it works. With Julius, the James twist is again invoked, and, as usual, the moment operates on two levels—but may be less fair than the other such usages. The reader enters Julius' mind after one of the murders (there are four), and on first reading, it appears to establish the time element. When the story is completed, however, the reader realizes that the scene has done more: it has established the peculiar emotional frigidity of this fillian:

Usually Julius Court fell asleep within minutes of turning out his bedside light. But tonight he turned in restless wakefullness, mind and nerves fidgety, his legs as cold and heavy as if it were winter. He rubbed them together, considering whether to dig out his electric blanket. But the bother of re-making the bed discouraged him. Alcohol seemed a better and quicker remedy both for sleeplessness and the cold.

He walked over to the window and looked out over the headland. The waning moon was obscured by scudding clouds; the darkness inland pierced only by a single oblong of yellow light. But as he watched, blackness was drawn like a shutter over that far window. Instantaneously the oblong became a square; then that, too, was extinguished. Toynton Grange lay, a faintly discerned shape etched in darkness on the silent headland. Curious, he looked at his watch. The time was eighteen minutes past midnight. (p. 181)

In this passage, there is none of the suffering or terror which Eleanor Maxie, Marion Bolam, or Sylvia Kedge undergo, and the tone is valid because Julius Court's crimes have been, unlike theirs, selfishly motivated. They kill from pain or for others; he kills to preserve his comfort. Perhaps this fact contributes to the heavy quality of *The Black Tower*, for the book is compelling but denser than the others.

V

It becomes clear, then, that P.D. James' insightful interest in human psychology provides quality thread for her fictional tapestries. Coupled with her ability to handle intricate plots, her mastery of the closed-circle technique, and her deft handling of various kinds of multiple point of view, the psychology explored yields well wrought, readable detective novels of excellent merit. Capable from the start, James is steadily achieving greater mastery of her craft, and will be--if she is not already--superior to Agatha Christie, with whom she is so often compared.

NOTES

[1] Jane S. Bakerman, "From the Time I Could Read I Always Wanted to Be a Writer," Interview with P.D. James, *The Armchair Detective*, 10:1 (January, 1977), p. 56.

[2] Interview with P.D. James by Jane S. Bakerman, May 19, 1976, London.

[3] Interview.

[4] Interview.

[5] Bakerman, p. 56.

[6] It should also be noted that the Dalgliesh-as-penetrator pattern serves also to underscore one of his chief characteristics--loneliness.

[7] Interview.

[8] There are two points at which the treatment may be said to be confusing, perhaps even unfair to the reader-problem-solver: the first occurs at the opening of the book, "Years later, when the trial was a half-forgotten scandal . . . ." (p. 7), and the second is similar, "In the years that followed when Eleanor Maxie sat quietly in her drawing-room...." (p. 216) Actually, as we learn in *A Mind to Murder*, she hasn't much time left to live.

ANNOUNCING A NEW PUBLICATION
DEVOTED TO THE SERIOUS STUDY
OF MYSTERY AND DETECTIVE FICTION!

THE JOURNAL OF RATIOCINATIVE RESEARCH

Published Quarterly or as Needed
Subscriptions $25 per year to Institutions,
$20 to Private Individuals

Edited and Published by
Euell Parrish, Ph.D.
Thorndyke Professor of Literary Ballistics
Popular Culture Department
West Dakota State Teachers College
221B Roman Policier Plaza
Flaxborough, East Carolina 00714

Some Topics to Be Covered in Early Issues:

* *The influence of Wilkie Collins on the novels of Mickey Spillane.*

* *The relative importance of Rodriguez Ottolengui and Burford Delannoy.*

* *Wadsworth Camp, the forgotten master.*

* *Fascism in the British Thriller, 1914-1925.*

* *Charles Dickens: a lost Wallace?*

* *Stylistic idiosyncrasies of Isabel Ostrander.*

* *John J. Malone for the defense: Craig Rice's use of legal procedure.*

* *The use of symbolism in the novels of Frank Gruber.*

* *The career of Peter Duluth viewed as a soap opera.*

* *Perry Mason and the new morality.*

* *Michael Avallone: trail-blazer.*

* *Henry Kane and the rebirth of regionalism.*

* *Political applications of the red herring.*

* *Special issue: trends in Icelandic detective fiction.*

* *Toothpick allegory in Ross Macdonald's novels (Part I).*

[Publicity release supplied by
Professor Parrish's agent, Jon Breen.]

FEAR AND LOATHING WITH THE LONE WOLF
By George Kelley

Imagine the unwary reader of the Destroyer, the Executioner, and other similiar vigilante heroes who specialize in killing Mafia members when confronted with "Mike Barry"'s LONE WOLF series. The response is an angry, "What the hell is this?"

"Mike Barry" is the pseudonym of Barry Malzberg, and that fact goes a long way toward providing an explanation. Malzberg is known for his dark and brooding science fiction; lately, with Bill Pronzini, he is known for his dark and brooding suspense novel *The Running of the Beasts* (Putnam, 1976; Fawcett, 1977).

The LONE WOLF series could be read as a parody of the heroic vigilante genre. Burton Wulff of the NYPD starts his hellish quest when his girlfriend is OD'ed by elements unknown to him. Wulff figures drugs and the international drug network is behind his girlfriend's death. So, in typical fashion, Wulff slaughters and kills his way across the country.

But the fact emerges that Wulff is insane. He is a man who needed an excuse to kill, and having found it, kills with machine-like efficiency through fourteen books characterized by all the personality and individuality of sausage links.

And, the men and women Wulff butchers are as crazy as he is. The unsuspecting readers of the LONE WOLF books find themselves in a bizarre, insane universe written in a style that is as unrelenting, as uncompromising, as a terminal cancer patient. Here's a sample:

> So Wulff had picked up the trail. Coming into Shreveport had been like coming into any of the hundred American cities that he had seen or passed in the months of his odyssey; once again he had been overwhelmed by the flattening of America, the gathering of all its cities into one, so that not only difference but any sense of partition had been obliterated. Now it was truly one country, all of it united by highways, loops, cloverleafs, abandoned downtown districts, hamburger stands, and the flat, blank surfaces of the screens of drive-ins coming up hard against the broken horizon; through that corpse where all cells had become one flowed the deadly silvery milk of heroin, which had first killed and was now embalming the corpse in clear frozen strips of hard poison, which yet glinted like something beautiful in the darkness. The vision of what drugs had done to his country was beautiful to Wulff only in the way that total disaster, utter corruption could be, but he did not think of this as slowly he pulled the folds of the tent which was Shreveport aside, looking for the place in which Cohen lived. When he found the man, he was going to kill him. (*The Killing Run*, pp. 53-54)

This is not the dull prose of lesser writers, yet it is not

the kind of prose you would want to read for an extended time. Call it an example of the literature of exhaustion: the tone is unrelenting in its depiction of death, insanity, disease, slime, and corruption. Reading the LONE WOLF series was an exercise in endurance, one that I won't be repeating in the near future. The books have a numbing quality, each book is another dose of novacane; the brutality, the killing, the degenerate acts fail to elicit any emotion after a while.

Malzberg is a talented writer, you can see that from the selection above, but he has a fatal flaw: Malzberg can't create a believable character.

Writers involve their readers by creating a sympathetic, believable character and minor interesting characters; as F. Scott Fitzgerald says: Action flows from character.

Without character, and Malzberg's writing is devoid of character, the writer can attempt to involve the readers by dazzling them with sparkling prose. A second strategy is to shock readers with explicit sex and graphic violence, hoping they'll continue reading for the thrill value.

But the simple fact is that not many readers will care what happens to Burton Wulff or any of the other zombies that populate Malzberg's work. Who is going to be engaged by zombies whose dialogue are as flat and obscure as a Harold Pinter play, whose motivations are death, suicide, and madness?

It's interesting that Malzberg's work is largely in the area of science fiction and pornography: two areas where character is subordinated to ideas and arousal. However, in the broader context of suspense fiction, character is essential and Malzberg is in deep trouble; the gimmicks and sleight of hand are not going to carry him in this genre.

Bill Pronzini and Barry Malzberg will be teamed up again in *Ride the Tiger* (Putnam) to be published later this year. Malzberg seems bent on working in the mystery and suspense genre; this gifted but flawed writer may be out of his league.

. . .

The LONE WOLF series, original paperbacks by Berkley written under the "Mike Barry" pseudonym:
```
#1  Night Raider.        1973
#2  Bay Prowler.         1973
#3  Boston Avenger.      1973
#4  Desert Stalker.      1974
#5  Havana Hit.          1974
#6  Chicago Slaughter.   1974
#7  Peruvian Nightmare.  1974
#8  Los Angeles Holocaust. 1974
#9  Miami Marauder.      1974
#10 Harlem Showdown.     1975
#11 Detroit Massacre.    1975
#12 Phoenix Inferno.     1975
#13 The Killing Run.     1975
#14 Philadelphia Blow-up. 1975
```

THE AVON CLASSIC CRIME COLLECTION
By Jeff Meyerson

Between September 1969 and November 1971 Avon Books published thirty-eight books in the Avon Classic Crime Collection series. They had a distinctive design of three colored stripes running diagonally across the front cover, spine, and rear cover that made them easily recognizable. Each book carried the following blurb inside: "The Classic Crime Collection is Avon's highly-acclaimed series of distinguished suspense novels. Some newly published, some long out of print, all make substantial claim to being standards of the genre." While this may be a slight exaggeration, the series did contain a number of classics, both new and old.

Unfortunately, little is known as to how and why the books were chosen, or how the conception of the series was brought about. Robert B. Wyatt, Avon's Editorial Director, wrote: "I'm afraid we can't be of much help to you, as most of the people involved in the program are no longer with Avon Books. I have been unable to locate a listing of the books published, but as I recall it totalled about two dozen titles. [!] The titles were chosen by the editorial staff at the suggestion of friends of the editors. A chief advisor was Shirley Glazer, wife of Milton Glazer who designed the MWA award-winning format for the series."

As to what type of books were chozen, there was quite a large variety of authors and types. About half were published by Avon for the first time in this series, the rest being reprints. The list included six Edgar winners: Best Novels *Beat Not the Bones* and *Death and the Joyful Woman*, and Best First Novels *The Horizonal Man*, *The Room Upstairs*, *Rebecca's Pride*, and *Florentine Finish*. One of the books, Hilda Lawrence's *The House*, was actually a novelette originally published with *Composition for Four Hands* in *Duet of Death*, but the others were all novels.

There were Golden Age classics, including *Trent's Last Case*, *The Red House Mystery* and *Death Under Sail*, and modern "suspense" novels like *Dead Corse* and *What Ever Happened to Baby Jane?*. There were successful first novels, like *The Rasp*, *It Walks by Night*, *A Puzzle for Fools*, *Blood Upon the Snow*, and *In the Last Analysis*; several authors' acknowledged masterpieces, like *One Man Show*, *The expendable Man*, and *The Lodger*; and modern works *Dead Cert* and *Accounting for Murder*. Hard-boiled addicts had *No Orchids for Miss Blandish*, *Green Ice*, and *Death in a Bowl*; espionage fans got *Ashenden* and *Legacy of a Spy*; Maigret devotees got two of his cases. One of the few lesser efforts was a middling Nero Wolfe case, *Where There's a Will*.

On the whole, then, it was a fine series, even though the selectors might have chosen a few more authors rather than having bour books by Hilda Lawrence and three by Philip MacDonald.

Why did it fail? Mr. Wyatt: "Initially, it was planned as a bookstore-only program, but it was so successful at first that newsstand distributors asked for copies. The series did not sell in this mode of distribution and in over-extension the Classic Crime Collection gained the reputation of failure and was abandoned. I'm fully aware that this is a frail explanation, but the vagaries of paperback distribution are odd, indeed." It's a shame, as the series brought many otherwise unavailable books back into print in an inexpensive, attractive format. Perhaps someday the series can be revived.

THE AVON CLASSIC CRIME COLLECTION*

PN221 Cornelius Hirschberg, *Florentine Finish* (9/69)
PN222 Dorothy B. Hughes, *The Expendable Man* (9/69?)
PN223 A. A. Milne, *The Red House Mystery* (9/69)
PN224 Mary Kelly, *Dead Corse* (9/69)
PN237 Dick Francis, *Dead Cert* (11/69)
PN238 Patrick Quentin, *A Puzzle for Fools* (11/69)
PN239 Hilda Lawrence, *Death of a Doll* (11/69?)
PN240 W. Somerset Maugham, *Ashenden* (11/69)
PN253 Vera Caspary, *Laura* (1/70)
PN254 Mildred Davis, *The Room Upstairs* (1/70)
PN261 Henry Maxfield, *Legacy of a Spy* (1/70)
PN262 E. C. Bentley, *Trent's Last Case* (1/70)
PN267 Ellis Peters, *Death and the Joyful Woman* (2/70)
PN268 Philip MacDonald, *The Rasp* (2/70)
PN277 Robert van Gulik, *The Chinese Bell Murders* (3/70?)
PN278 C. P. Snow, *Death Under Sail* (3/70)
PN282 Henry Farrell, *What Ever Happened to Baby Jane?* (4/70)
PN283 John Dickson Carr, *It Walks by Night* (4/70)
PN286 Charlotte Jay, *Beat Not the Bones* (5/70)
PN287 James Hadley Chase, *No Orchids for Miss Blandish* (6/70)
PN293 Rex Stout, *Where There's a Will* (5/70)
PN294 Michael Innes, *One Man Show* (6/70)
PN311 Celia Fremlin, *The Jealous One* (7/70)
PN312 Emma Lathen, *Accounting for Murder* (7/70)
PN320 Hilda Lawrence, *Blood upon the Snow* (9/70)
PN321 Donald McNutt Douglas, *Rebecca's Pride* (8/70)
PN322 Anne Chamberlain, *The Tall Dark Man* (8/70)
PN323 Philip MacDonald, *Murder Gone Mad* (10/70)
PN328 Helen Eustis, *The Horizontal Man* (9/70)
PN330 Georges Simenon, *Maigret in Vichy* (10/70)
PN335 Amanda Cross, *In the Last Analysis* (11/70)
PN336 Marie Belloc Lowndes, *The Lodger* (1/71)
PN337 Raoul Whitfield, *Death in a Bowl* (12/70)
PN339 Georges Simenon, *Maigret and the Headless Corpse* (3/71)
PN355 Hilda Lawrence, *A Time to Die* (5/71)
PN373 Raoul Whitfield, *Green Ice* (7/71)
PN382 Philip MacDonald, *The Rynox Murder* (11/71)
PN387 Hilda Lawrence, *The House* (9/71)

* The dates are those given on the copyright page, which do not always follow the numerical order. Those with question marks are those I haven't actually verified.

THE NERO WOLFE SAGA
Part III
By Guy M. Townsend

[*The Second Confession* [June 1949], published in 1949.]

The Second Confession [June 1949] was published in 1949. Baring-Gould lists it incorrectly in his chronology as "The Gun With Wings." This novel virtually devies brief summation. Wolfe is hired by a corporation president, James U. Sperling, to prevent the marriage of his daughter to a gangster lawyer named Rony who may or may not be a communist. Arnold Zeck calls and warns Wolfe off the case, but Wolfe naturally persists. So, at 2:24 one morning, Zeck has a couple of his thugs fire 192 rounds "from an SM and a tommygun" into the plant rooms atop the brownstone, doing at least $40,000 worth of damage. Wolfe and Archie journey out to the Sperling country place for a conference, and while they are there Wolfe's car is used to run over Rony in the driveway. The local police are called in and regard it as murder until one of Sperling's company officers, who was visiting at the time, confesses to having borrowed Wolfe's car and run over Rony by accident in the dark. The police, and Sperling, are satisfied with the accident theory, but Wolfe doesn't buy it. And neither, for that matter, does Zeck. Wolfe eventually exposes the murderer, with the reluctant and mutually distasteful assistance of two high-ranking men in the American Communist Party.

This is one of the most complex and fast-paced episodes in the Saga to date, and a major reason for this is Arnold Zeck. Zeck, you will recall, made his first appearance in the Saga in *And Be a Villain*, though he had phoned Wolfe twice before regarding cases of which Archie has left us no record. In the episode now under consideration we learn that Wolfe and Zeck have had another close encounter since *And Be a Villain*. Archie mentions that Rony was observed entering Bischoff's Pet Shop and Wolfe sharply asks him what he knows about the shop. Archie replies, "Nothing to speak of. I only know that last November when Bischoff came to ask you to take on a job, you told him you were too busy and you weren't, and when he left and I started beefing you told me that you were no more eager to be committed for Arnold Zeck than against him. You didn't explain how you knew that that pet shop is a branch of Zeck's far-flung shenanigans, and I didn't ask." In *The Second Confession* Zeck's role rises from the level of a menacing force generally off-stage, to that of a major character. Zeck's ultimatum to Wolfe, Wolfe's disregard of it, and Zeck's reaction to Wolfe's disregard have already been mentioned. It was the attack on the plant rooms which caused Wolfe to once again break his rule against leaving the house on business: "He was not really smashing a precedent. It was true that he had an unbreakable rule not to stir from his office to see anyone on business, but what had happened that night had taken this out of the category of business and listed it under struggle for survival."

In *The Second Confession* Wolfe gives a lengthy (5 pp.) and detailed account of his knowledge of and dealings with Arnold Zeck, from his first inkling that Zeck existed more than a decade before: "I first got some knowledge of him eleven years ago, when a police officer came to me for an opinion regarding a murder he was working on. I undertook a little inquiry through curiosity, a luxury I no longer indulge in, and found myself on a trail leading onto ground where the footing was treacherous for a private investigator. Since I had no client and was not committed, I reported what I had found to the police officer and dropped it. I then knew there was a man such as X, and something of his activities and methods, but not his name." It was not until Zeck's first call to Wolfe eight years later, in 1946, warning him off a case, that Wolfe pursued the matter any further: "For my own satisfaction I felt that I needed some information. . . . Not wishing to involve the men I often hire to help me, and certainly not Mr. Goodwin, I got men from an agency in another city. [This contradicts his statement in *And Be a Villain* that he had hired some of Bascom's men for the job. Unless, of course, Bascom's agency has offices in another city.] Within a month I had all the information I needed for my satisfaction, including of course X's name, and I dismissed the men and destroyed their reports. I hoped that X's affairs and mine would not touch again, but they did."

The similarity between Zeck--X, in the above quotations--and Professor Moriarty is really quite striking. Wolfe says "He has varied and extensive sources of income. All of them are illegal and some of them are morally repulsive. Narcotics, smuggling, industrial and commercial rackets, gambling, waterfront blackguardism, professional larceny, blackmailing, political malfeasance--that by no means exhausts his curriculum, but it sufficiently indicates its character. He has, up to now, triumphantly kept himself invulnerable by having the perspicacity to see that a criminal practicing on a large scale over a wide area and a long period of time can get impunity only by maintaining a gap between his person and his crimes which cannot be bridged; and by having unexcelled talent, a remorseless purpose, and a will that cannot be dented or deflected." Zeck maintained this gap through means of a gigantic criminal network, at the bottom of which is the workaday criminal (A), who has contact only with his immediate superior (B), who in turn has contact only with *his* immediate superior (C), who in his turn has contact only with *his* immediate superior (D). "Here we near the terminal. D knows X and how to get to him. . . . I don't know how many D's there are, but certainly not many, for they are selected by X after a long and hard scrutiny and the application of severe tests, since he knows that a D once accepted by him must be backed with a fierce loyalty at almost any cost. I would guess that there are very few of them and, even so, I would also guess that if a D were impelled, no matter how, to resort to treachery, he would find that that too had been foreseen and provisions had been made. . . . You see where X is. Few criminals, no A's or B's or C's, even know he exists. Those few do not know his name."

Wolfe describes what he must do if he ever decides to, or is forced to take on Zeck: "I shall move to a base of operations which will be known only to Mr. Goodwin and perhaps two others; for it is not a fantasy of trepidation, but a painful fact, that when he perceives my objective, as he soon will, he will start all his machinery after me. He has told me on the telephone how much he admires me, and I was flattered, but now I'll have to pay for it. He will know it is a mortal encounter, and he does not underrate me--I only wish he did. . . . I shall expect to win, but there's no telling what the cost will be. It may take a year, or five years, or ten. . . . Once started, I'll have to go on to the end. So the cost in time can't be estimated. Neither can the cost in money."

But that confrontation is not destined to take place in *The Second Confession*. On the contrary, the murder of Rony, who was one of Zeck's men, and the willingness of the police to accept the accident theory, ironically put Wolfe and Zeck on the same side--both want the murderer exposed and punished. Zeck sends Wolfe a package containing $50,000 in cash and then telephones him and says, "I don't need to explain why I decided to reimburse you for the damage to your property. Do I?" Wolfe answers, "Yes", but he already knows that it's for tracking down Rony's killer. Zeck says, "Rony was an able young man with a future, and he deserves to have his death investigated by the best brain in New York. Yours. I don't live in New York, as you know. Good-by and good luck." After this call Wolfe repeats once again his order that Archie forget Zeck's name. "The reason is simply that I don't want to hear his name because he is the only man on earth that I'm afraid of. I'm not afraid he'll hurt me; I'm afraid of what he may someday force me to do to keep him from hurting me."

Wolfe decides to put Zeck's money to good use: "After what happened Sunday night [the shooting up of the plant rooms, which actually happened early Monday morning]--we'll be prepared for contingencies. If we ever meet him head on and have to cut off from here and from everyone we know, we'll need supplies," so he instructs Archie, after setting aside some for expenses, to "take the remainder to a suburban bank, say somewhere in New Jersey, and put it in a safe deposit box which you will rent under an assumed name." Wolfe spends $15,000 of the $50,000 getting information, and Zeck sends another package around containing--surprise!-- $15,000, which Archie puts with the rest of the money in a safe deposit box in "a certain city in New Jersey." When it's all over Zeck calls Wolfe, congratulates him, and remarks, "In view of the turn events took the damage your property suffered is all the more regrettable."

Besides being replete with references to Zeck, *The Second Confession* contains a plethora of other Saga developments, though only a relatively few of these relate directly and exclusively to Wolfe. At one point Sperling says to Wolfe, "Apparently you have no equal," upon which "Wolfe grunted, trying not to look pleased. 'There was a man in Marseilles [sic]--but he's not available and he doesn't speak English.'" Is this just flummery? Wolfe later says of himself, "I am congenitally tart and thorny." One aspect of Wolfe's personality which I have inexcusably overlooked up 'til now is his reading habits. In the case at hand he is reading an unnamed book by Laura Hobson. This may not, however, be a true reflection of his tastes, since the book is not in his own library but is selected from Sperling's shelves to while away the hours that Wolfe must remain at that gentleman's country estate. Of the physical Wolfe we learn that he is wearing a bright yellow shirt and yellow socks!, and Archie at one point refers to Wolfe's "eighth of a ton," which indicates that Wolfe has undergone a significant weight loss since we were last given his poundage. Lastly, Archie again tells us that "Wolfe's wits leave him when a woman cries."

ARCHIE ::: Archie appears to be something of an accomplished diver, he mentions going to high school in Ohio, and he is drinking gin in this episode (Good man). He also admits to the bad habit of leaving the key in the car "when I'm parking it on the private grounds of a friend or a client," and he mentions another habit which we have encountered before--"I have a rule never to travel around on homicide business without a shoulder holster." With something in it, of course. Archie slaps a right-wing, Paul Harvey type radio commentator around a bit for making some snide remarks about Wolfe over the air. Wolfe's impression of this fellow is that, to quote Archie, he "would have been more at home in Hitler's Germany or Franco's Spain." Finally, Archie says he "quit using logic on women the day I graduated from high school."

WOLFE & ARCHIE ::: On the subject of Communism Wolfe speaks for himself and Archie when he agrees with someone who has asserted that Communism is "intellectually contemptible and morally unsound." Archie, who appears to regard communists as reptiles of some sort, says "I wouldn't put anything beneath a Commie." [Neither would I, but then I wouldn't put anything beneath a capitalist, either.] Wolfe's affection for Archie, and Archie's reciprocation of same, is indicated by Wolfe's birthday gift to Archie of a caribou hide bag and Archie's obvious pride and pleasure in it. Of his relationship with his boss Archie says: "One reason I like to work for him is that he never rides me for not acting the way he would act. He knows what I can do and that's all he ever expects; but he sure expects that." And, of course, he gets it; in the case at hand Archie's performance is so exemplary as to rate a "satisfactory" from Wolfe. But Wolfe also shuts Archie out of one aspect of the case, telling him to go to bed as Wolfe is expecting a caller. "That had happened not more than twice in five years. Once in a while I get sent out of the room, and frequently I am flagged to get off the phone, when something is supposed to be too profound for me, but practically never am I actually chased upstairs to keep me from even catching a glimpse of a visitor. 'Mr. Jones?' I asked." More about this mysterious Mr. Jones later.

OTHER REGULARS ::: Lon Cohen makes a brief appearance; Archie says, "Lon had been rank and file, or maybe only rank, when I first met him, but was now second in command at the *Gazette*'s city desk." Theodore is mentioned, and Fritz is ever present but unobtrusive. Archie's "old friend and even older enemy" Purley Stebbins shows up briefly, and the Bascom Detective Agency is mentioned in passing. Andy Krasicki, who took Theodore's place during the illness of the latter's mother in "Door to Death", "had come in from Long Island and was in charge" of clean up and repair after the great orchid massacre. No mention is made of the duration of his earlier stay at the brownstone, nor of what alteration in the condition of Theodore's mother's health made it possible for him to leave her side [did she recover, or did she die?]. Lewis Hewitt, Wolfe's rival orchid fancier, comes to call on Wolfe regarding plants, and another flower man, G. H. Hoag, is mentioned, I think for the first time, as a fellow flower fan/friend with Wolfe and Hewitt.

Several of our former acquaintances from Westchester County make appearances. Of District Attorney Cleveland Archer Archie says, he "was a little plump and had a round face, and he could tell a sonstituent from a tourist at ten miles, but he wasn't a bad guy." Also, there is Lt. Con Noonan of the State Police, who "would never forget how I had helped Wolfe make a monkey of him in the Pitcairn affair." And there is "Ben Dykes, head of the county detectives," who "had been a Westchester dick for more than twenty years, and all he cared about was doing his work well enough to hang onto his job, steering clear of mudholes, and staying as honest as he could."

We learn a good deal more about Doc Vollmer in this episode. "Doc's home and office were on our street, toward Tenth Avenue, and over the years we had used his services for everything from stitching up Dora Chapin's head to signing a certificate that Wolfe was batty." Actually, it was Dora's neck that needed stitching, not her head. Archie speaks of Doc's short legs and his spectacles. Doc Vollmer is clearly liked by the inmates of the brownstone; Archie says that in speaking to Doc Wolfe used "the tone he uses only to the few people he really likes," and elsewhere Archie remarks, Doc "trotted out, making me move fast to get to the front door in time to open it for him. His habit of leaving like that, as soon as he had all he really needed, was one of the reasons Wolfe liked him." Another reason may possibly be found in the following: "He accepted Wolfe's offer of a bottle of beer, as he always did when he called in the evening."

Saul, Fred and Orrie all show up, and Archie has a few remarks about each of them. We learn [is this the first time?] that Saul has a wife and children (exact count and sex not specified), and Archie says that "one difference between Saul and me is that I sometimes have to look twice at a thing to be sure I'll never lose it, but once will always do for him." Of Fred and Orrie Archie says they were not alike. "Fred was some bigger than Orrie. When he did anything at all, walk or talk or reach for something, you always expected him to trip or fumble, but he never did, and he could tail better than anybody I knew except Saul, which I would never understand. Fred moved like a bear, but Orrie like a cat. Orrie's strong point was getting people to tell him things. It wasn't so much the questions he asked. As a matter of fact, he wasn't very good at questions; it was just the way he looked at them. Something about him made people feel that he ought to be told things." Here's an interesting item involving the three of them having drinks with Wolfe and Archie: "a bourbon and soda for Saul, and gin fizzes for Orrie and me, and beer for Fred Durkin and Wolfe. Straight rye with no chaser was Fred's drink, but I had never been able to talk him out of the notion that he would offend Wolfe if he didn't take beer when invited." Finally, in this episode Wolfe asks for, and gets, assurances from Saul, Fred and Orrie that, if he (Wolfe) comes into possession, through them, of evidence which will convict the killer but decides to withhold it, they will not spill it themselves.

We are also introduced for the first (and, I think, last) time to Ruth Brady, a female operative whom Archie employs for a subterfuge.

Another character who makes his first appearance in *The Second Confession* is the above mentioned mysterious "Mr. Jones." This gentleman, whose name was *not* Jones, was an informer of some sort who Wolfe had used twice before but took pains not to let Archie meet. Archie says, "I had never seen the guy, but I knew two things about him: that it was through him that Wolfe had got the dope on a couple of commies that had sent them up the river, and that when you bought from him you paid in advance." In this instance "Jones" gets paid $15,000 for providing Wolfe with detailed accounts of several secret meetings of higher ups in the American Communist Party, which Wolfe uses to force the Communists to assist him in unmasking the murderer.

PHYSICAL ASPECTS ::: No address is given for the brownstone this time, but it is said to be "on West Thirty-fifth Street nearly to Eleventh Avenue." Inside the office the globe and "the big yellow couch in the corner" are mentioned, and Archie tells us that Wolfe's chair is "warranted safe for a quarter of a ton. Archie tells us his "guns are in my second drawer but not loaded," and then he speaks of "the gun I keep on my bed table." The West 35th St. folks have now become a two car family, possessing a sedan and a convertible, both of unspecified make and model, which are kept in a garage on 11th Ave. The one-way panel in the front door is mentioned again, and the orchid count is given at 10,000 this time. Finally, Theodore's room is on the roof in a corner--no further specifics given--so it is lucky he wasn't shot up during the massacre.

ROUTINE AT THE BROWNSTONE ::: Archie says, "when I am out and expected home it is not customary for Fritz or Wolfe to put on the chain bolt except on special occasions." This is a change from earlier episodes. The doorbell answering business is also in flux again, as Archie says Fritz answers it until nine in the evening, after which it is Archie's job (Fritz having changed into his old slippers at that hour). But the early morning routine remains the same--"Ordinarily I have my breakfast in the kitchen with Fritz and Wolfe has his in his room." Elsewhere Archie remarks that "in the morning my custom is not to enter the office until after my half an hour in the kitchen with Fritz and food and the morning paper."

ODDS & ENDS ::: This department is rather short this time around, except for this cryptic allusion to an unchronicled case half a dozen years before: "The locksmith soaked me $8.80 for eleven keys. That was about double the market, but I didn't bother to squawk because I knew why: he was still collecting for a kind of a lie he had told a homicide dick six years ago at my suggestion. I think he figured that he and I were fellow crooks and therefore should divvy."

"The Gun With Wings" [August 1949], published in *Curtains for Three*, 1950.

THE STORY ::: This time Wolfe and Archie are approached by Margaret Mion, recently widowed wife of Metropolitan Opera tenor Alberto Mion, and her lover Frederick Weppler, who engage Wolfe to prove that neither of them murdered the late Alberto. Mion's death had been accepted as suicide by the police, but Margaret ("Peggy") and Fred, who had withheld vital evidence from the police, know it to be murder and wish to remove every vestige of suspicion of each other before they take the step of getting married. A fairly interesting tale, with a tad more detecting in it than the average Wolfe short story.

WOLFE ::: Wolfe says "I am neither an Astraea nor a sadist," and he uses the not too common word splenetic; otherwise the big word business remains in the doldrums. But we do encounter a number of Wolfe's idiosyncrasies on this outing: "Wolfe absolutely cannot stand people who don't eat enough"; "During meals Wolfe excludes business not only from conversation but also from the air"; "For a while he just sat, and then began pushing his lips out and in, and I knew he was doing hard labor. . . . I have seen him sit there like that, working for hours on end." And here are a couple of new items: "I could tell from the line of his lips, straightened out, that the next item on the agenda was one he didn't care for"; "Wolfe was drumming on his desk blotter with a paperknife, scowling at it, though I had told him a hundred times that it ruined the blotter."

It is in "The Gun With Wings" that we first learn that Wolfe has begun to ration his beer consumption. "I want another bottle of beer," he says, and Archie replies thusly: "'Nuts. You've had five since dinner.' I didn't bother to put much feeling into it, as the routine was familiar. He had himself set the quota of five bottles between dinner and bedtime, and usually stuck to it, but when anything sent his humor far enough down he liked to shift the responsibility so he could be sore at me too." Wolfe's disappointment at the inadequacies of the English language when referring to an unnamed murderer are brought up by Archie: "As Mr. Wolfe says, the language could use another pronoun."

ARCHIE ::: Archie uses the word apodictical, but this is counterbalanced by a lapse in grammar elsewhere: speaking of fingerprints he says, "none are hardly ever found on a gun that are any good." His notebooks are once again in evidence. Here's a familiar item: "I have a rule, justified by experience, that whenever a killer is among those present, or may be, a gun must be handy." Archie earns high praise again from Wolfe: "I acknowledged the tribute with a careless nod. It does not hurt my feelings when he says, 'Satisfactory,' like that."

OTHER REGULARS ::: Theodore is mentioned but does not appear. The same is true of Fritz and Lily Rowan, though Archie tells us a bit about them: of Fritz he says that he's "the chef and house overseer who helps to make Wolfe's days and years a joy forever almost as much as I do"; and of Lily he says that they occasionally go to the opera together. "My old friend and enemy, Sergeant Purley Stebbins" shows up but doesn't do anything.

The only other regular to receive any attention is Cramer. We are given some more information about his appearance and his temperament: "For nine months of the year Inspector Cramer of Homicide, big and broad and turning gray, looked the part well enough, but in the summertime the heat kept his face so red that he was a little gaudy. He knew it and didn't like it, and as a result he was some harder to deal with in August than in January." Cramer and Wolfe get into a noteworthy row in this episode--"I have sat many times and listened to that pair in a slugging match and enjoyed every minute of it, but this one got so hot that I wasn't exactly sure I was enjoying it." One last thing re Cramer--we encounter a contradiction of earlier remarks regarding his smoking habits: "Cramer stopped chewing his cigar. He never lit one." In fact, he used to light them, but Archie appears to have forgotten. Later in the Saga Archie goes so far as to say that he's never seen him light one, which is also incorrect.

PHYSICAL ASPECTS ::: The orchid count is again given as 10,000; it seems to have stabilized at that level. When he is not carrying them, Archie keeps his guns in "the back of the third drawer of my desk," which is a change. The arrangement of the furniture in the office is clarified somewhat when Archie says that when he is seated at his desk he has a full face view of whoever is sitting in the red chair.

ROUTINE AT THE BROWNSTONE ::: The doorbell answering routine has changed again: it rings at 9:00 in the evening and Archie says, "I was so curious to have a look that I went to answer the door instead of leaving it to Fritz." But Archie has previously told us that he always answered it from 9:00 onward because that was when Fritz put on his slippers.

MYSTERIES FOR SALE

By Queen, R. MacDonald, Fleming, Christie, MacInnes, Stout, Le Carre, Ambler, Aarons, Nick Carter, Gardner, Eberhart, and many others

```
Paperbacks    5¢-30¢    S. C. Owen
Hardbacks     55¢-80¢   P. O. Box 343
DBC Triples   75¢       Moraga, CA  94556
Mystery Mags  30¢
```

Send 25¢ for list of over 400 books.

MYSTERY*FILE

SHORT REVIEWS BY STEVE LEWIS

Richard Forrest, *The Wizard of Death* (Bobbs-Merrill; c. 1977; 188 pp.)
    Connecticut residents will get a kick out of this inside view of state gubernatorial politics. When the nominee Randolph Llewyn is assassinated at a political rally, it appears that writer Lyon Wentworth's wife is the next target. Bea Wentworth is a state senator and has a great deal of influence over who the next nominee will be.
    The Chamber of Commerce is not likely to be pleased with some of the ground uncovered during the course of the investigation, including the hangouts of several motorcycle clubs lobbying against the helmet bill and the sleazier side of Hartford's massage parlor district. The whole business is pretty unlikely, and one fears that it's quite superficial but it reads quickly and it is fun to indulge your fantasies. (C)*

Arthur Maling, *Schroeder's Game* (Random House; c. 1977; 204pp.)
    Emma Lathen's distinguished banker-detective John Putnam Thatcher has had his special niche in the mystery field to himself for quite some time. This, however, is now the second book involving Brock Potter, of the specialized brokerage firm of Price, Potter and Petacque. This is misadventure in the world of high finance, on a grand scale.
    Murder reveals the soft underbelly of a Phoenix-based hospital billing company that Potter's firm has underwritten. The boom in Arizonan land values and reinvested profits has come to an end. While there is less detection than in Miss Lathen's books, kidnappings and hired killers do provide considerably more action and suspense. Wall Street must still be shaking. (B)*

Sara Woods, *The Law's Delay* (St. Martin's; c. 1977; 223 pp.)
    Antony Maitland defends another client whose claim it is that when she found the body she picked up the gun without thinking. The trial comes, strangely enough, in the middle of the book, leaving a large gap in this sad human interest story to be filled in later.
    It's an old-fashioned kind of story, very formal, very stodgy, with a lot of questions that have to be asked and answered, yet there are unexpected overtones of gangsterism entering in. Unfortunately I find Maitland and his entourage of family and friends nearly insufferable bores. (C-)*

Rex Burns, *The Farnsworth Score* (Harper & Row; c. 1977; 197 pp.)
    Gabe Wager is a detective working for Denver's Organized Crime Division. While the previous book in this series (*The Alvarez Journal*, reviewed in *TMF*'s Preview Issue) was sound enough as a procedural, it did rather overemphasize the dullness of police routine. This one, on the other hand,

---

* Reviews so marked have appeared earlier in the *Hartford Courant*.

crackles with excitement from end to end, as Wager reluctantly goes underground as a dope-pushing Chicano in an effort to nab one of the state's top dealers, using an arsenal of guns stolen from an army reserve unit as bait.

Assignment in the narcotics division may not have the glamor of working for Homicide, say, but it's probable that more lives are at stake. Burns neatly contrasts the beauty of the Colorado countryside with the dirty business going on in its darker corners, with the unhealthy stench of shit making law enforcement a job for only the few who can take it. We get the added challenge of a whodunit as well, since Farnsworth's previous bust was mysteriously fouled up. Is there a leak in the division? (A)*

Paul Ferris, *High Places* (Coward, McCann & Geoghegan; c. 1976; 1st published in Great Britain under the title *The Detective*; 1st American edition, 1977; 176 pp.)

Commander Crocker, head of the intelligence branch of Scotland Yard's Metropolitan Police, accidentally uncovers a liaison between the Home Secretary and a thirteen year old call girl. In his mind Sir Harry Blancagnell is guilty, not so much of bad morals, but of bad judgment. A man widely touted as the next prime minister should not make such an error.

This is not so much a detective story as a gloomy Orwellian novel of faltering British traditions. Crocker is suddenly hemmed in by the walls of a watchful government that refuses to act upon his information. It's a more complicated problem than the corruption behind Watergate, however, since the alternative of removing Blancagnell and his policies of moderation during a summer of labor turmoil would only escalate the trend toward violent confrontation. Should the dirt be simply brushed away? Ferris is not warning us of the future, but telling us about the present, with a worried eye toward the narrowing edge we have in controlling our own civilization. (A)*

Whit Masterson, *Hunter of the Blood* (Dodd Mead; c.1977; 211 pp.)

A schizophrenic priest with a message threatens Rome with nuclear disaster during the Pope's annual Easter sermon. Gus Gamble is the only man who knows that plutonium stolen from a Nevada nuclear fuel facility has actually been smuggled into the Vatican, but he's frustrated at every turn by bureaucratic disbelief.

Gamble is a priest working Las Vegas blackjack tables when he's persuaded to reassume his former duties as head of security for the AEC. He's what might be called a born manhunter, that rather unlikely sort of individual who can miraculously turn up clues that hundreds of other investigators have already passed over. Unfortunately his intuitive conclusions are too often only partially based on hard evidence.

Masterson doesn't quite succeed in arguing that one man surrounded by massive manpower in the computer age can be the only one to come up with the right answers, but he will cause a few palms to start sweating as the big boom approaches. (B)*

Mike Jahn, *The Quark Maneuver* (Ballantine 25171; c. 1977; 1st printing, March 1977; 188 pp.)

Add yet another liberated lady to the growing list of feminine sleuths we have seen recently. Her knowledge of karate helps save the lives of a pair of cops at the mercy of two blacks with automatic rifles underneath the Queensboro bridge and involves her in their subsequent pursuit of a Quark-carrying madman capable of bringing on World War III. What's a Quark? Only a portable surface-to-air missile powerful enough to bring down the plane carrying Hua Kuo-feng, the premier of China, into New York City for a UN summit conference.

Her name is Diana Contardo, and she runs a pretty fair restaurant on 59th Street, but she soon finds that romance and adventure are much more fun. I concur whole-heartedly and hope that this won't be the last we see of the delightful Miss Contardo, truly a beauty with brains, as she tackles more cases with her new friend Lieutenant DiGoia, who is not so old as he first appears. I do have one gripe, though, about an ending that's both too loose and yet too tightly plotted. See if you don't agree. (B)

Robert Lee Hall, *Exit Sherlock Holmes* (Scribner's; c. 1977; 238 pp.)

Now it can be told. The famous retirement as a beekeeper on the Sussex Downs was but a pretense, part of Sherlock Holmes' strategy employed against his alter ego of evil, the notorious Professor Moriarty, who not surprisingly also did not perish at Reichenbach Falls.

In all the cases he previously recorded for us, Watson never reveals much information about the early days of his famous friend. In fact, for the most of their life together he never greatly inquired. However, in the great detective's final days Watson did finally learn the whole story. Through a legacy left him by his grandmother, a tin box of Watson's writings stored away until this year, Robert Lee Hall now claims to be able to reveal the truth.

Watson has the spotlight for most of the book, for Holmes has mysteriously disappeared during the growing international crisis foreshadowing World War I, and with the able assistance of the now adult Wiggins, he does quite creditably as a detective, discovering for the first time Holmes' secret laboratory and the other deceptions perpetrated by Holmes over the years. Loose ends from many tales are deftly tied together, and all the mystery surrounding the life of Sherlock Holmes is magnificently cleared away by the revelations preceding the final confrontation scene, revelations which, I promise you, are designed to test your imagination to the utmost.

A must for Holmesians, but if it makes any difference, I didn't believe a word of it. Nor could I put it down. (A-)

Lesley Egan, *The Blind Search* (Doubleday; c. 1977; 175 pp.)

Lawyer Jesse Falkenstein is faced with the nearly impossible task of returning a nine year old girl to the only parents she knows, a kindly couple who brought her up after she was abandoned with them by her mother, but who still have no legal right to hold her. They had hoped for six years that the mother had gone for good, then she suddenly returned on a Sunday morning to claim her child only to then disappear with her without a trace. In effect, a legal kidnapping.

Compulsively readable in spite of the hokum about spiritualism and psychic phenomena. It doesn't really interfere all that much. As a police procedural (Sergeant Clock is Falkenstein's brother-in-law), it's wrapped up more neatly than real life would allow, but who cares? It's nice to be satisfied by a surprise ending that doesn't come out of a hat. (A)

Bill Pronzini, *Blowback* (Random House; c. 1977; 149 pp.)

As you may very well already know, this begins with the nameless private detective as he waits for the report on his lungs to come through. It is a tumor, he knows that now, but is it malignant? He means to sweat it out alone over the weekend, but a call for help from a friend takes him a short way out of himself, up into the mountains, to mix a little fishing with business.

There are six men at the camp, and one woman, which is just the right mixture to provoke a murderous amount of jealousy and hatred, but how do a stolen Oriental carpet and a lone peacock feather enter in? Pronzini enjoys doing a tough-edged version of classical detection, and he may surprise a few who don't pay close attention; but he adds something more--a rare view of someone confronted with and facing his own mortality, analyzing his life, comparing it with those of the pulp heroes he emulates. The fact that he, and others, still read their adventures makes certain their kind of immortality, and while I can't tell you what the doctor's report says, even without a name there is now another private eye to be added to the list of those who may in time be forgotten by many--but not by all. (A minus)

Edward S. Aarons, *Assignment Afghan Dragon* (Fawcett Gold Medal P3527; c. 1976; 1st printing, June 1976; 192 pp.)

The folks at Fawcett have quit numbering the books in the Sam Durell series, but at a guess there must be close to fifty of them by now. I must confess to never have become very interested in Durell, although recently he has occasionally become more suitably reflective in terms of who he is and what he's done to survive in his long years of service for K Section. I think the young mod-looking chap on the cover is an imposter.

What you can count on in a Sam Durell adventure are the exotic glimpses of parts of the world you really wouldn't care to visit in person, no matter how tempting Aarons makes them sound. For example, this one begins with a brutal murder in the middle of the Dasht-i-Lut, which we all immediately recognize as the Iranian desert near the border with Afghanistan, and then we're taken on an intensive CIA-sponsored tour of the high and low spots of both countries. All that's missing is an ancient jewelled dragon that war-mongers in three major powers have made into a symbol of national pride, and Durell is caught looking.

Lots of action, most of it petering off into the predictable and perfunctory. (C)

Ian Kennedy Martin, *The Deal of the Century* (Holt, Rinehart & Winston; c. 1976; 1st published in US, 1977; 170 pp.)

It's hard to picture the playboyish Inspector Regan as the leading detective in the "Sweeney," Scotland Yard's famed Flying Squad. Not that he doesn't finally crack this case of an assassinated oil sheikh in admirably ruthless fashion, but frankly he seems too long preoccupied with interbranch politics and his prowess with the female half of the species. It takes some poking around in London's finest bordellos and a stay at one of the plushier Riviera hotels before he uncovers the truth of the affair, which then suddenly explodes into violent action and reaction. It could easily be mistaken for real dramatic content. (C plus)*

James Patterson, *The Thomas Berryman Number* (Ballantine 25552; c. 1976; 1st Ballantine edn, April 1977; 218 pp.)

This is the inside story of an assassination, told in semi-documentary fashion by the newspaper reporter who helped break the case. Actually nobody else wanted to take a trip to a Long Island mental hospital to listen to the ravings of a madman, but included in his ramblings was the name of the murdered black mayor of Nashville, killed while making a run for the U.S. Senate.

The MWA voted this the best first novel of the year, but I thought the format was disastrous. With most of the story known in advance, suspense is hard to come by. I felt twice removed from the story, and nobody came around to fill in the plotholes. Even the portions told in first person lacked any immediate impact.

I could say some good things too, like how the narration is nicely interspersed with entertaining bits of homely Americana, from Texas to New England, but read it for yourself. What it lacks in suspense it makes up for in the fascination of watching unfold something you know is going to happen, and it may grab you more than me. (B minus)

Mark Washburn, *The Armageddon Game* (G.P. Putnam's Sons; c. 1977; 352 pp.)

A small-time underground explosives expert is offered a million dollar assignment to construct--well, what kind of bomb would be worth that kind of money to build? The mystery is who's behind it, what's their plan, and how can they be stopped?

You may never feel safe in your easy chair again. Nobody asked the rest of us before the first bomb was dropped, and nobody's asking now. This will make you shake for a while, and all the more when you realize that Washburn has written himself into a melodramatic version of Mission Impossible that he can't get out of. We won't always be this lucky. (B)*

David Linzee, *Death in Connecticut* (McKay-Washburn; c. 1977; 245 pp.)

Where have the protesters of the 60's gone? They've vanished completely, swallowed up into the faceless American scene, selling out to the Establishment. The smart ones, anyway.

So discovers Arthur Lavien, a dropout from Columbia,

returning home after three years on the road. The year is 1971, the revolution is not in sight, and his sense of failure is overwhelming. Suicide is making others say they're sorry. But surprise--could his ex-girl friend and his father be trafficking together in drugs? Two packages full cause quite a scramble, not a very funny one, and Arthur's world and beliefs are turned upside down.

This one's about a loser, about children who grow up in empty houses, and about parents who cannot always cope with their own problems. The locale is Hartford and its immediate suburban environs, but Linzee brings the wandering revolutionary home in striking fashion, whereever. (A minus)*

Brian Garfield, *Recoil* (Morrow; c. 1977; 335 pp.)
The author of *Death Wish* tries another approach this time. When Fred Mathieson finally decides to stop running from the mob and turns to fight instead, he makes it clear that killing is one thing he will not do, not even in self-defense.

Gut feelings for justice and revenge are aroused to high intensity when Mathieson turns from defensive maneuvers to full-fledged attack, but fighting organized crime on its own level takes an enormous amount of effort and manpower, and the strength of the final blow is weakened by the long buildup. Worth reading for Garfield's carefully worked out solution, even though it won't fully satisfy non-realistic expectations that were raised too high. (B plus)*

Carter Brown, *The Stripper* (Signet S1981; c. 1961; 1st ptg., August 1961; 127 pp.)
She's billed as Deadpan Delores, the girl who says it all from the neck down. Yes, indeed, she could easily provoke an interesting evening of intimate conversation. Lt. Al Wheeler unfortunately has a one-track mind and wants only to read between the lines.

What it's about, if it matters, is a suspicious suicide, a lonely-hearts club and a strip joint. It'd be unworthy of anyone to compare Wheeler's activities to anything resembling actual police procedure, but if you like incessant wisecracks and incredibly sexy dames permeating your detective fiction, this might serve to soothe that ache in the mushy part of your mind. (C)

Donald MacKenzie, *Death Is a Friend* (Houghton Mifflin; c. 1967; 230 pp.)
I think the reason I bought this was because one of the crooks in this ill-fated crime caper is a stamp dealer by profession. (I used to collect the things before I discovered that once hinged into an album there's nothing you can do with them.) Three men brought together by greed are splintered apart by distrust, jealous hatred--yes, there's a woman involved--and fate's fickle finger.

MacKenzie is not a particularly good writer, but he's often an effective one. Except for the ending, which made no sense at all, this is a pretty fair example of the destructive effects inherent in some human relationships. Nothing about stamps, however. (C plus)

H. C. Bailey, *The Red Castle Mystery* (Crime Club; c. 1932; 312 pp.)

Introducing lawyer Joshua Clunk, who daringly skirts the edge of the law but, unlike Perry Mason, knowingly takes the cause of the underworld. His problem here is to find the connection between the death of a client, a London fence found face down in the contents of a smashed bottle of leeches, and the disappearance of the ten year old heir to an ancient family castle in Strathland.

Clunk is an annoying giggler with fluttering hands, addicted to sweets and hymn singing, filled with the kind of religious fervor you would not think compatible with one of his profession. Lots of false trails along the way, and ominous hints that people aren't telling all they know. The great number of shady characters involved tends to overwhelm the plot and in fact produces most of the mystery, one that a good scorecard would help keep straight. Good reading on an idle summer's day. May the quiet misty countryside of rugged English moors always exist! (B minus)

Frances Crane, *The Cinnamon Murder* (Random House; c. 1946; 244 pp.)

I'm fairly sure that part of the reason mystery readers are attracted to Frances Crane's novels is the colorful set of titles she endowed them with. That, plus the fact that someone who picks one up to read knows that there will be a mystery involved, one that will be thoroughly puzzled over before being solved in the end, and that love will find its way.

This one takes place in New York, just as Pat and Jean Abbott are about to return home to San Francisco. This leaves Jean with just one hat, and believe me, don't we hear about that, and how inappropriate it is for "sleuthing." Why she is allowed to tag along, I don't know, since Pat is the detective in the family, and Jean misses most of everything, even those clues that might be considered of a feminine nature--clothes, fingernail polish, that sort of thing.

Unlike the Norths, there's no comedy involved, but there are more red herrings than you can flail an oar at. Jean tells the story, but Pat tells her nothing, and so after becoming accustomed to being left in the dark with her, I admit that I was caught unawares when suddenly the lights came on, this time with the guilty party firmly in Pat Abbott's grasp.

Feather-headed sort of stuff, but OK. (C)

Andrew York, *The Fascinator* (Crime Club; c. 1975; 179 pp.)

James Bond is not dead. It's taken me a while to discover it, but Jonas Wolde, with many years of service to British Intelligence already behind him, is the logical successor. He's not as flamboyant a character perhaps, but Wilde is very much a deadly adversary, and he possesses quite the same remarkable fascination to women. Trained agents they may be, but soon enough they become sexual objects to be toyed with as well. Fascinating.

Actually he's retired at the beginning of this one, fed up, torn loose, and lost in the soothing touch of Spanish sangria. A puzzling task presented by Israeli Intelligence under duress reawakens his faculties, however, and when he agrees to become the bodyguard of an Arabian potentate yachting in the Mediterranean, no amount of clever plotting or overwhelming firepower can sway him from the job he was hired for. He's an indefatigable one-man task force, but after he's trapped by an explosion in an underwater cavern with the wounded prince and his number one consort, all you can do is hold your breath during yet another attempt at escape. (B plus)

Bill Knox, *Rally to Kill* (Crime Club; c. 1975; 183 pp.)
It was interesting to note that this is Knox's 22nd mystery novel, not including those appearing only in England or those written under two or three pseudonyms. He's a competent writer, as well as prolific, but as yet he's gained no great reputation to go with all those books. This one's probably typical of his Thane and Moss series.

Those two particular gentlemen are inspectors for the Glasgow C.I.D., and what they're involved with this time is a dead girl who was strangled after she was murdered, a peeping Tom, a whiskey investment company and the hind of rallies put on by car enthusiasts. Thane mixes it up with more action than does Commander Gideon, for example, but otherwise it's tempting to say that this is a pale plaid imitation of that other series. Nonetheless it's a solidly written procedural that should not be ignored by fans of the form. (C)

George Harmon Coxe, *The Glass Triangle* (Dell 81 w/map; c. 1940; 240 pp.)
This is vintage Coxe, written while he was still fresh from toiling a decade or more for *Black Mask* and other pulps. I've never really been sure why he switched to Kent Murdock as the detective in his early novels, rather than continue with Flashgun Casey, as they seem to blur in my mind into the same character, the tough successful news photographer who continually finds himself involved in murder.

In this one Murdock introduces the sister of an old friend to a Hollywood crowd in town for a movie premiere, then feels it his obligation to protect her when the director, unliked by all, is murdered in his hotel room. There's no moral consideration involved, just a newspaperman's curiosity and what he owes on a promise to a friend.

So OK, call him medium-boiled. Coxe's heroes are people who stick up for each other, easily inspire trust and confidence, and who are maybe just a little soft at heart.

A piece of glass is the only tangible evidence Murdock has after the corpse disappeares and his photographic plates are stolen, but only the careful reader will spot the additional clues Coxe slips in. I did name the killer, but that's about all. The only question left unanswered is why the supremely detestable director was along on the junket in the first place. (B)

VERDICTS

(MORE REVIEWS)

Gregory Mcdonald, *Fletch* (Avon, 1976, 252 pp.; orig. 1974) and *Confess, Fletch* (Avon, 1976, 270 pp.)

    Anyone who wins two Edgars with his first two books, as Gregory Mcdonald has (Best First Novel and Best Paperback Original) must be doing something right. Both *Fletch* and *Confess, Fletch* are damned good books--funny, witty, and thoroughly delightful.

    Irwin Maurice Fletcher, known as Fletch, is an excellent reporter. While operating undercover in an attempt to break the drug traffic on a California beach, he is hired by millionaire Alan Stanwyk to murder him for fifty thousand dollars. He claims he is dying of cancer and wants his wife to get his three million dollar insurance policy but Fletch is skeptical, so he starts digging into Stanwyk's life while continuing on the drug case. His very felicitous lying enables him to get the information he needs as time runs out on the two cases. I was able to figure out the solution, but this is an extremely well-written and exciting book that holds the interest throughout its length. It is written largely in dialogue, which Mcdonald is very good ad; only Fletch's two ex-wives strain the credulity.

    Confess, Fletch begins with Fletch, no longer a reporter, arriving in Boston to try and locate some paintings stolen from his Italian fiancee's family. The first night he returns to his borrowed apartment and finds the nude body of a murdered girl. He tries to fend off the police, in the person of Inspector Francis Xavier Flynn, as he tries to find the connection between the respectable Horan Gallery and the stolen paintings. If the plot is slightly less good than its predecessor, the book would be worth buying for Flynn--a truly memorable, warm, likeable and intelligent character, who almost brings about Fletch's comeuppance. Let's hope the two return soon. (Jeff Meyerson)

Simon Brett, *So Much Blood* (Scribner's, 1976; $6.95.)

    Charles Paris, middle-aged actor who made his debut in *Cast, In Order of Disappearance*, is back. He takes his whiskey guzzling, skirt-chasing self to Edinburgh where, for want of any better employment for his moderate talents, he puts on his one-man show based on the work of Thomas Hood as a part of the Edinburgh Festival, or, rather, On the Fringe of same. Paris is thrown into intimate contact with numerous theatrical types a generation his junior, and when one of them is murdered on stage with a dagger that was not supposed to be real he decides to exercise the detective skills he first discovered in *Cast* to run the murderer to ground. But before it is over he becomes personally involved with several of the suspects and tries to wash his hands of the whole thing. It is too late, though, and the murderous mess grinds inexorably on to its conclusion, leaving two more corpses in its wake.

    Paris takes several wrong turns, but he does at last arrive at the solution. Not, however, ahead of the reasonably astute reader, who should spot the murderer, if not the motive, well before the end. Nevertheless the story is an interesting one and well told, the settings are attractive and stimulating, the characters are well drawn, and Charles Paris is an engaging, believable and sympathetic character. Encore. (Guy M. Townsend)

Arthur Morrison, *Best Martin Hewitt Detective Stories*, selected, with an introduction, by E. F. Bleiler (Dover, 1976, $3.00)

Martin Hewitt was one of the early "Rivals of Sherlock Holmes". Like the Master, he is a private detective, whose exploits are recorded by a friend, in this case a man named Brett. Unlike Watson, however (at least if the nine stories in this collection are typical), Brett does not appear regularly in the stories themselves. Hewitt lacks the eccentricities and bizarre interests and habits of his greater contemporary, coming across as a rather commonplace individual whose only remarkable aspect is his ability to make sense out of problems which baffle everyone else. Hewitt's very blandness is a weakness of the stories, since it means that the ingenuity of the plots has that much greater a load to carry. And these plots are, by and large, quite inferior to those of the Holmes Canon. This does not mean, however, that this collection is not worth reading. Quite the contrary. The stories suffer mainly by comparison; were there no Holmes, Hewitt would stand much higher in our estimation. And since the Holmes stories are limited in number, it is comforting to know that there are entertaining, if conventional Martin Hewitt stories to fall back on.

The best stories in this collection are "The Stanway Cameo Mystery" and "The Case of the 'Flitterbat Lancers'". The first of these, concerning the disappearance of an immensely valuable piece of ancient art work, is the best by far; indeed, Hewitt's detection is worthy of Holmes himself. The second revolves about a cypher even more ingenious than The Dancing Men.

Dover's collections of the "Best Stories" of the early writers in our genre are all welcome, since many of these stories would not otherwise be generally available, and this volume is especially so since it reproduces in facsimile the original magazine pages, complete with numerous illustrations. Several artists are represented, by far the best, to my prejudiced eye, being Sidney Paget. (Guy M. Townsend)

Mary Roberts Rinehart, *The Circular Staircase* (introduced by Phyllis A. Whitney, bibliography by Jan Cohn, illustrations by Darrel Millsap. Del Mar: University Extension of the University of California at San Diego/Publishers Inc, 1977; originally serialized in *All Story*, 11/07-3/08; first book publication Bobbs-Merrill, 1908. 249 pp., $5.95.)

The Mystery Library continues its slow, inexorable march towards the nineteenth century with its third volume. This is the first book in this series to be written by a woman and also the first to be written before the First World War; it is also the worst volume yet. Rinehart, for those of you unfamiliar with her, was a popular novelist of the first part of the twentieth century--her career ran from

1905 to 1955, more or less. Mysteries or criminous works were about a third of her output.

Our heroine is Rachel Innes, a propertied middle-aged woman. When her brother's children, Halsey and Gertrude, need to be entertained during the summer, Innes finds a country manor, owned by Paul Armstrong, president of the Traders' Bank. When the Innes brood moves into Sunnyside (the name of the manor) mysterious events start to happen. Iron bars crash through walls in the middle of the night. Strange apparitions terrify the servants. Arnold Armstrong, Paul's son, is found murdered at the foot of the circular staircase. Evidence--or what passes for evidence--disappears and reappears. The Traders' Bank fails, and this is the beginning of a long sub-plot of offstage financial intrigues. Can sense and order be made out of these disparate dangers?

Here we have a mystery, but not a novel of detection. Most of the characters (or at least the admirable ones) react instead of act--everyone is pulled along by what passes for vast, mysterious forces. There are clues, but nothing is done with them--they act as MacGuffins, to be lost whenever the plot slackens off. No use is ever made of them, because if they *were* used, we would not have our intrepid heroine blithely beginning the series of coincidences that pass for a conclusion. I doubt many people today would be entertained by a heroine who is unable to face perils on her own; Innes does little except to act as narrator. (There is also a touch of racism, centering around the character Thomas Johnson, the gardner; but this is not enough to bother me.) *The Circular Staircase* is a *bad* book, perhaps of interest to the antiquarian or the scholar, but with little to recommend it to the casual lover of thrills.

The appendices, though, are magnificent. Whitney's introduction is good, but unexceptional; the main text, though, has some very fine period work by Darrel Millsap, an artist The Mystery Library should continue using. There are extracts from Rinehart's autobiography and from a book of interviews with writers, *A Writer Observed*; a list of film versions of *The Circular Staircase* and *The Bat* (a play based on *The Circular Staircase*), all compiled by the admirable Robert E. Briney. Jan Cohn, whomever she may be (I gather she is a librarian at the University of Pittsburgh) did the bibliography, and also wrote an introduction to Rinehart's first story, which is also included here. Finally, there is a reproduction of two pages from the notebook Rinehart used to record her sales, and reprints of a 1908 review of *The Circular Staircase* (from the *New York Times*) and her obituary in a 1958 *Publishers Weekly*. It's a good job despite some errors (the captions to the two pages of the sales log are mixed up, and I find it odd that Rinehart's first story can be found while the date of it cannot--it was in *Short Stories*, which is a popular (and quite common) pulp; this is indeed the critical edition, so it's a shame that all those hours of effort were used to garnish a novel that should have remained buried in the past. Story C-, Appendices A. (Martin Morse Wooster)

Gore Vidal, *Matters of Fact & Fiction: Essays 1973-1976* (Random, 1977.)

Some of you may be surprised to see me praising a book by a noted mainstream author, and a book of his essays on top of that.

But Gore Vidal is no stranger to the mystery field. Under the pseudonym of "Edgar Box," Vidal wrote three entertaining mysteries: *Death in the Fifth Position* (1952), *Death Before Bedtime* (1953), and *Death Likes It Hot* (1954).

In *Matters of Fact & Fiction*, the essays range all over the political and literary landscape. But I particularly want to recommend the excellent essay on E. Howard Hunt.

The early works of E. Howard Hunt have become collectors items not just for genre collectors, but for general bookcollectors as well. Surprisingly, it is not only Hunt's Watergate notoriety but his skill as a writer that is a prime reason for this flurry of collecting.

Vidal does a nice job tracing Hunt's early works that were mainstream and noting the drift toward suspense and action novels as Hunt's career in the CIA brought him actual espionage experience.

Also, very interestingly, Vidal compares Hunt's works across series; Hunt wrote under several pseudonyms, chiefly, Gordon Davis, John Baxter, Robert Dietrich, and David St. John.

With all the current interest in E. Howard Hunt, Gore Vidal's essay is an excellent guide to Hunt and his work. (George Kelley)

Ed McBain, *Even the Wicked* (American Library, March 1977.)

Newscaster Zach Blake receives a note telling him his wife did not drown accidentally as he believed. Blake and his daughter Penny go back to Martha's Vineyard, where the drowning occurred a year ago. Blake looks for the writer of the note and finds her murdered. Penny is kidnapped and Blake told to leave town if he wants her returned. He does leave but comes back with Penny, more than ever convinced that his wife was murdered. The plot is not well developed, perhaps because the story is so short (132 pages). Only fair. (Myrtis Broset)

Ed.McBain, *Where There's Smoke* (Ballantine, July 1977)

McBain introduces a new character, Benjamin Smoke, a retired police lieutenant. Smoke acts as a private investigator although he has no license to do so, and therefore cannot charge for his services, but does quite well accepting gifts. Smoke's theory is that it is all-right to lie, as long as it does him some good, and he goes merrily along lying all the way.

Smoke is seeking a case he cannot solve, the perfect crime. This book deals with his fifth case, a corpse stolen from a mortuary. This corpse is returned but another is stolen and the mortuary attendant murdered. Smoke has no client but keeps working on the case, hoping this will be the one he can't solve. While tracking down the missing body Smoke adopts a bird, witnesses a Satanist wedding, meets some weird characters, and keeps one step ahead of the regular police, much to the annoyance of Homicide Detective O'Neill.

The plot is weak, the suspense is nil, and the reader will guess the ending. Ex-Lieutenant Ben Smoke is what makes the book worth reading--to walk with him through the pages of this book is a delight. (Myrtis Broset)

Robin Moore, *The Terminal Connection* (Ace Books, Sept. 1976)
When the Masters Security computer equipment fails to stop a jewelry showroom theft, Paula Masters knows they must be able to prove the failure was not the fault of the company, or she will have to recompense Slayton Jewelry for the loss, as this has been the policy of the company since it was founded by Paula's deceased husband. This loss would cause Masters Security to become bankrupt.

Two members of the Board of Directors try to force Paula to resign as President, but she resists, hoping her men will solve the puzzle before the next meeting of the Board.

Keith Stuart, banker, is kidnapped and Paula is drawn into the matter by the man's wife. The banker is released after a ransom has been paid, and later killed.

Paula has a friend on the police force and they work together to solve the jewelry theft and murder with the aid of the Masters Security Chief Investagator and Computer Programmer. The police officer is convinced Stuart was murdered by his wife but Paula does not agree.

The book deals with wire tapping, industrial espionage, kidnapping, murder and adultery in a fast-paced, intriguing manner. Not to be missed. (Myrtis Broset)

Mike Curtis, *The Savage Women*, Mark Andrews, *Body Rub*, J.C. Conaway, *The Deadly Spring* (Leisure Books, $1.50 each.)
"Fanatical feminists use sex to lure men to their death"; "massage parlors were a front for prostitution . . . . and worse"; "a deadly chemical released the savage nature of everyone in town."

These are the flamboyant captions, splashed over lurid pictorial covers, of the latest sex-and-sadism paperback originals published by Leisure Books.

The Savage Women features a group of beautiful women obsessed with hatred for all men. They roam the streets and the singles' bars, picking up men, luring them into no-escape situations. Then they strike with animalistic ferocity, utilizing razor-edged instruments for castration and murder.

It is a narrative filled with graphic sex descriptions, including lesbian sequences and brutality galore. Somewhere between the gory lines there is a hidden message: women of the world--unite. We will no longer tolerate man's dominance, rape and other multitude of sins against womanhood. We will take the offensive and punish man.

But the message gets lost in the ghoulish relish with which the seductive women execute their grim punishments. There is also a male head to the gang, a mad albino, and it is not clear why he, a sadistic man, should be obeyed instead of getting his just deserts.

Pitted against the murderous feminists is a very tough police detective, reminiscent of Dirty Harry, only more extreme in his unorthodox, rough tactics.

There is very little rhyme or reason to the action and

a great deal of amorality by heroes and villains. It is a work that makes no pretenses other than appealing to the basic instincts of its readers.

Body Rub is another badly written, explicit narrative. It boasts one of the most complicated plots ever. The protaganist is an investigative reporter assigned to do a series of articles on New York's massage parlors. He gets entangled with the Mafia and a cult of devil worshippers. Soon gangsters, prostitutes, cultists and policemen bump into each other in various areas of the sinful metropolis. Four or five girls, all beautiful, are assassinated, and it is impossible to keep track of who killed whom for what.

It is a mixture of sexual exploits, some basic detection and a touch of the occult. There is a feeble attempt to illustrate the workings of a daily newspaper, and somewhere along the line there is an "impossible murder"--the victim discovered in a room locked from the inside.

The Deadly Spring had a true potential. The action takes place in a small, rural town in West Virginia, located near a military base. Secret experiments in chemical warfare are being conducted in the base.

A succession of earthquake tremors shakes the town, and the author describes various characters, in short vignettes, as they are affected by the sudden tremors. It is quite a beguiling method of introducing the dramatic personae simultaenously.

The quake caused the breakage of vials in the army laboratory, and a deadly drug was released into the town's water supply. It affected the minds of everyone who drank the water--releasing savage and sadistic urges, normally kept hidden under the veneer of civilized society.

Now there is a second series of rapid episodes--brutal and bloody. A soldier stabs his wife repeatedly with a rifle bayonet. A group of children attack their spinster teacher with sticks and slowly beat her to death. A repressed daughter fatally strikes her domineering mother with sewing shears. An underpaid chef shoves his employer's face into a boiling cauldron.

Then there is a homosexual rape and murder, a passionate incest sequence, a pack of wild wolves on the rampage and a flock of chickens attacking savagely an elderly farmer.

When it is all over, one realizes with disappointment that actually the author had nothing to say. The reader was mesmerized for a while by what seemed to be an intriguing premis, overwhelmed by the rapid pace, shocked by the graphic violence, but is left with an empty feeling and a nagging suspicion that the whole work is a hoax.

In summation, the three X-rated books will not enrich anyone's literary palate. However, they possess one virtue: perusing them will keep many a reader away from kinky mischief. (Amnon Kabatchnik)

James Anderson, *The Affair of the Blood-Stained Egg Cosy* (McKay-Washburn, 1975, 250 pp., $6.95.)

Fans of the typical English house party mysteries of the 1930s, rejoice--the Golden Age is back! James Anderson's book has it all, including a list of characters and a plan of the house and, as the worried Inspector Wilkins puts it: "Foreign envoys. International jewel thieves. American millionaires. European aristocracy." Though he keeps saying he is not sanguine, Inspector Wilkins manages to unravel the many-stranded plot and sort out a head-spinning series of complications, with the help of a (semi-)amateur assistant. Guests at the Earl of Burford's stately home include his diplomat brother Richard and some foreign envoys trying to work out an agreement; an American oil millionaire interested in the Earl's fabulous gun collection and his wife; a strangely enigmatic and beautiful Baroness; society bore Algy Fotheringay, who gets his just deserts; an early-Christie type ingenue, down on her luck; and possibly the Wraith, a society jewel thief. As might be expected Anderson has a lot of fun with this, though he does it affectionately without playing for laughs. There are ultimately two murders, which naturally take place during a violent thunderstorm when no one stays in his room. *Egg Cosy* has all the joys, and some of the weaknesses, of the classic mysteries of the Golden Age. The latter include a few poorly delineated characters and the convention of having a culprit launch into a long and detailed confession upon being accused, rather than clamming up and sending for a lawyer. On the plus side are the situation itself, the marvelously convoluted plot and its multi-part situation, somewhat reminiscent of early Queen. There is even a secret passage! If the events of the night in question and the whereabouts of all the people and guns are just about impossible to keep straight, that's all part of the game. There are indications of a possible sequel at the end--I hope there is one, as it's a fun book, well worth reading. (Jeff Meyerson)

Keith Laumer, *Fat Chance* (Pocket, 1975; originally published as *Deadfall* by Doubleday, 1971; 190 pp.)

Although *Fat Chance* is Laumer's first strict mystery (a second, *Cop Trouble*, should be released soon), he handles it like an old pro. And why not? Keith's been writing detective oriented science fiction for years (*Night of Delusions, Trace of Memory, Plague of Demons*). The characters in his SF books have been very private eye like in appearance and manner, so the excellence of *Fat Chance* is not surprising, at least not to this reader.

Fat Chance is an obvious and intentional imitation of Chandler's work. Keith's Los Angeles investigator, Joe Shaw (I wonder if his middle initial is T) is Philip Marlowe, no doubt about that. Joe's a wise cricking, heavy drinking loner who does a lot of ankle hanging at the office and solves chess problems at home.

The good thing about *Fat Chance* is that Laumer doesn't try to improve on Chandler, he tries to continue the exploits of P. Marlowe, and due to Laumer's ability to master the Chandler style, *Fat Chance* could easily fall in line as the eithth--ninth if you count *Trouble Is My Business*--Marlowe adventure.

This particular novel, although it contains elements of all the Chandler books, reminds me most in tone of *The Little Sister*. Like *The Little Sister*, it puts great emphasis on humour.

The story deals with Shaw's employment by Lou Anglich, a retired strongarm. Lou wants Shaw to follow a twenty-five year old trail in search of a waif he once befriended and lost track of in a foster home.

Shaw's search leads him to the Prendergast mansion where two lovely sisters reside (one Shaw suspicions might be Lou Anglich's little Anya) along with their aged and ailing mother and a suspicious uncle. In grand Chandler tradition Shaw is lied to, misled and used as a punching bag by two hoods "who were probably to small to be ex-Ram linebackers."

Some may feel Laumer's book smacks far too close to the originals, but for Chandler fans who wish to see the adventures of Philip Marlowe continued, it's a feast served up by a man who loves and knows the work of possibly the greatest detective writer of them all. *Fat Chance* is virtually a love letter to Chandler and Philip Marlowe. A+ (Joe Lansdale)

Georges Simenon, *Maigret and the Black Sheep* (Harcourt, Brace, Jovanovich, $6.95), Nicholas Freeling, *The Bugles Blowing* (Harper & Row, $7.95.)

Jules Maigret and Henri Castang both work for France's Police Judiciaire, but any similarity between the two stops there. Maigret, that great-hearted bear of a man, larger than life, patiently sucking on his pipe or sipping a calvados in the local brasserie while he absorbs the atmosphere of a milieu, was created by Georges Simenon in 1931 and appeared regularly until the author's retirement in 1972. Castang, an efficient if featureless cog in the investigative bureaucracy of an unnamed provincial city, is the newest creation of Nicolas Freeling, whose better known series character was the late Inspector Van Der Valk of the Amsterdam police. Put together the new Castang novel and a recently translated Maigret and you have a measure of how the European police novel has evolved over the past few years.

Maigret and the Black Sheep first appeared in France in 1962, but from internal detail it might as easily date from 1932 or 1952. The murder of a retired cardboard-box manufacturer in a middle-class Montparnasse apartment building brings Maigret into confrontation with the dead man's wife, daughter and son-in-law, all three of whom seem to Maigret to be hiding something. His efforts to penetrate their common secret take the form of foot-slogging routine rather than the usual near-mystical osmosis by which he blends into his surroundings until he comprehends them. The book as a whole, though smooth to read, lacks the substance and bite of the best Maigrets and seems almost like a work of the 19th century when compared with Freeling.

The Bugles Blowing opens on a stifling Sunday afternoon with a government official's phoned confession to Castang that he has just walked into an orgy involving his wife and teen-age daughter and the artist who was painting the wife's portrait. He has killed all three. The murderer's high position leads everyone to expect a whitewash, a plea of temporary insanity followed by a brief sentence to a country-club-like psychiatric institution. But this killer seems obsessively determined to force the government to execute him. The movement of the story is ponderous, painfully precise, like the French criminal justice system which is its subject, and Freeling captures both the nobility and the nonsense in the ritual behavior of the system's functionaries. Without suspense or surprise, we are made to march to the gallows with a murderer whose execution becomes both more unthinkable and more inevitable with each chapter.

The strength of this novel lies in its slow accumulation of details--legal, literary, culinary and sheerly human --reflecting countless aspects of French life including the polarization caused by the Arab-Israeli conflict and the existence of a number of professional terrorists used by the government for political assassinations. One would never find such a wealth of contemporary minutiae in the classically uncluttered policiers of Simenon.

When a British police officer in *The Bugles Blowing* speaks of "those awful Maigret books" in which the French policemen become exceptionally sharp after about four Pernods," he may or may not be speaking for Freeling. But there is definitely a new form of European sensibility at work in the police novel, and readers with a taste for it will not want to forget Freeling or Castang. (Francis M. Nevins, Jr. This and the following review are reprinted from the *St. Louis Globe-Democrat*, 13-14 March 1976 and 18-19 September 1976 respectively.)

John Ball, *The Eyes of Buddha* (Little, Brown, $7.95.)

"You don't look very much like Sidney Poitier," a nightclub singer tells Virgil Tibbs in the fifth novel about the black Pasadena detective; and indeed he doesn't. John Ball's character is not the aggressive black action-hero of the three Poitier films but more like an English gentleman of the old school, suddenly gifted with dark skin and transported from an Agatha Christie country manor to the freeways of southern California. His clothes and manners are impeccable, his taste in art and music sophisticated, his speech slightly stilted as is the speech of most of the characters in Ball's police novels. Nothing could be further removed from the sick and vicious California cops one finds in the novels of Joseph Wambaugh.

In Virgil's latest case a scout troop finds the decomposing body of a young woman in a remote sect-on of Oak Grove Park. The police speculate that it may be the body of a wealthy industrialist's daughter who vanished without a trace a year before, and the old file is reopened. Medical evidence soon proves that the two women are not the same but the missing-person case stays open and Tibbs is assigned to both matters. His search for the hidden connection between the fates of the two young women takes him halfway around the world to tiny Nepal, in the shadow of the Himalayas, where he finds clues to the solution.

Unfortunately the book is not a complete success. Ball has tried simultaneously to write an authentic police procedural and an old-fashioned detective novel; the trouble is that the two genres collide at crucial points. The investigative detail is meticulously accurate and real members of the Pasadena police department appear as characters. But at the same time the famous detectives of fiction--Holmes, Mr.

Moto, Arthur Upfield's Inspector Napoleon Bonaparte--are also treated as real people, and one of them, Stuart Palmer's school-teacher-sleuth Hildegarde Withers, is given a cameo role in this novel. Information that routine police questioning would ordinarily reveal is kept artificially hidden so that Tibbs can deduce it later from the nuances of suspects' statements. The final plot-twist completely scrambles our picture of the relationship between two of the book's major characters. But despite its flaws this is a highly readable book, with Ball's enthusiasms for classical music and Oriental art and travel to exotic corners of the world all worked carefully into the fabric. No friend of Virgil Tibbs will want to miss his latest adventure. (Francis M. Nevins, Jr.)

Leslie Charteris, *The Saint in New York* (Curtis, nd; orig. pub. 1935; 224 pp.)

The Saint, Simon Templar, is brought to New York by William Valcross's offer to pay him one million dollars to destroy the crooks that kidnapped and murdered his son. Templar is indestructible as he almost single-handedly breaks up the gang that has New York in its powerful grip, as he works his way upwards in search of "The Big Fellow". The book and the Saint have a delightful charm and easy-going, nonchalant manner, along with more serious undertones (but not too serious). Though his exploits are improbable, and though the experienced reader should figure out his adversary before he does, the Saint is a fine companion who's worth getting to know. (Jeff Meyerson)

Elisabeth Sanxay Holding, *The Blank Wall* (DBC, nd.; Simon & Schuster, 1947.)

One of the nice extras that come with acquiring old volumes issued by the Detective Book Club is the fact that they often introduce you to "new" writers. Recnetly, I happened upon Elisabeth Sanxay Holding's *The Blank Wall* in this fashion and was delighted to discover a good, solid writer I had been overlooking.

The mystery in this story is not very mysterious; the reader knows from the outset who committed the killing, but the book is fascinating nevertheless. Holding here lives up to her reputation as an early practitioner of the psychological mystery by centering her tale around a few crucial days in the life of Lucia Holley. Mrs. Holley is a woman who has spent her life being protected by father, husband, and son--or so it seems. She identifies herself as a housewife and, until the period of the book, is quite content with that role. Her main motivation throughout is to nurture and protect the people in her charge, particularly her daughter and aged father. But we meet Lucia in unusual times. The setting is during World War II, and her husband is fighting in the Pacific. We watch this upper middle-class woman cope with the infringements of the war itself and with murder.

At first glance, then, Lucia Holley seems like an angry feminist's nightmare: she is unself-confident, full of self-blame, seemingly dependent, eager to follow the orders of any man handy, and unable or unwilling to think of herself as genuinely attractive. Indeed, she sometimes seems younger than her eighteen-year-old daughter. But for both Lucia and the reader, that first glance is not fully revealing. The book explores whether or not Lucia *can* cope with violence on both a personal and international scale, and Holding points that out early:

> She had the resourcefulness of the mother, the domestic woman, accustomed to emergencies. Again and again she had had to deal with accidents, sudden illnesses, breakdowns. For years she had been the person who was responsible in an emergency. She had enough physical strength for this job. What she lacked was the spirit for it. (DBC edition, p. 11)

Her attempts to find that spirit and exert her strength provide the interest and even the excitement in this book. Lucia must fend off the police, deal with the encroachments of the black market, come to know and evaluate a man with criminal ties who finds her extremely attractive--and do all this in the face of the constant demands of her family, none of whom must know fully what is going on. For the first time, she must sort out a divided loyalty and she must deal with the fact that her obligations to her family make her a very real danger to a man, an outsider in every sense, whom she has come to respect and, to a considerable degree, to care for. And, of course, she has to continue to balance those ration points! In the hands of Elisabeth Holding, these tensions produce an interesting and compelling story.

The chief strength of the book lies in Lucia's genuine reality. She never abandons her role as nurturer, but she does recognize the new alliance and reevaluate an old friendship (with her black maid, Sibyl, a fine characterization). Holding keeps the study within the bounds of realism by allowing changes to grow naturally in Lucia's character--she learns, for instance, to tell her children flatly that she has a right to some life of her own--without violating her central loyalty to her role as wife and mother. The final result is sound. The book is a good one, and of specail interest to readers whose feminist consciousnesses have been raised. Once again we find that the messages regarded as new have often been there, waiting for us all along. (Jane S. Bakerman)

Frank Gruber, *The French Key Mystery* (Avon 91, 1946; orig. 1940; 262 pp.)

Frank Gruber was a mainstay of the pulps, grinding out over 600,000 words a year for many years. In 1940 he turned out this, his first detective novel, in a week, and it was a big success (a film was made with Albert Dekker and Mike Mazurki). It is the first of fourteen books with quick-thinking, fast-talking Johnny Fletcher, the world's greatest book salesman, and his brawny sidekick Sam Cragg. Fletcher and Cragg are locked out of their hotel room for non-payment of the bill; when they climb in through the window of the next room they find a dead body in their bed clutching an extremely valuable gold coin in his hand. From then on it's one fast moving complication after another, as Fletcher must clear himself of murder, find the real killer, and solve the mystery of the coin. Despite a few improbabilities of plot, *French Key* is pulp writing at its best, with a briskly moving plot, breezy dialogue, and lots of action. It also offers an interesting picture of New York in 1939, when a nickel could buy a hamburger at a greasy spoon, as well as a ride on the subway, and a suite at the Waldorf went for as little as twenty-five dollars a day. (Jeff Meyerson)

Suzanne Blanc, *The Green Stone* (Lancer, 1966; orig. pub. by Harper & Row, 1961.)

We know who the murderers are in the first chapter, in a way; not necessarily their names, that doesn't matter, for they are minor characters; they only start the chain of events.

The catching of the killers is of great concern, of course, to the admirable Indian detective, inspector Menendes of the Tourist Section, and at first seems so to the plot, but later on the reader finds he or she is mainly concerned with events connected with the emerald.

The inhabitants of a small Indian village in Mexico become aware of the riches to be gleaned from an automobile wreck in the vicinity. Three of the villagers, thereafter, take it upon themselves to influence the turn of events by causing a wreck. The resort to the simple, expedient, though somewhat drastic, maneuver of shooting a motorist in the head with a rifle. After the inevitable wreck, one of the killers, without the knowledge of the other two, takes an emerald ring from the hand of the dying woman tourist.

The stone is later purchased by a guide, who, when it gets too "hot", surreptitiously sells it to our damsel, who will, in a little while, be in very much distress.

There is little in the book that doesn't advance the plot or build character, and there are good character studies too; especially those of the Inspector and the guide.

Most of you will spot the key to the puzzle early on, but no matter, it is better this way, and probably what the author had in mind, as it is an obvious clue. Then you can watch and wonder if, and when and how it will come to the Inspector's attention. It's a joy to watch him "tie up the threads." There is one thing more to be said about this book. It won an Edgar. Read it if you can. (Robert M. Williams)

Samuel Spewack, *Murder in the Gilded Cage* (Simon, 1929)

The famous playwright (*Boy Meets Girl, Kiss Me Kate*) wrote two mystery novels in the late twenties that are reputed to be minor works.

Murder in the Gilded Cage is minor, but it's an agreeable and highly readable work that is not without interest today.

This is Spewack's second and last mystery. It's dedicated to his wife and collaborator, Bella.

Cage starts in New York City, but soon moves onto the yacht *Mary Rose* which heads straight for Cuba where most of the action takes place. Very few mysteries have been set in Cuba--especially in these days of unfriendly relations.

The narrator is an ex-newspaperman turned press agent named A. A. Abbott (shades of Fulton Orsler!) whose style of expository opening betrays a familiarity with the work of S. S. Van Dine.

The official detective is Ben Smith of the Richmond Police Department, currently on assignment to the Cuban police force due to increasing American tourism. He is colorless but competent and has been successful in the past.

The "Great Detective" is Boris Sergeivitch Perutkin, a former member of the Russian secret police who was forced to flee his native land at the time of the revolution. He is able to render considerable assistance to the police when the wealthy and eccentric divorcee Mrs. Henry Breese is murdered.

Perutkin is far from infallible, and does have several serious setbacks, including a misguided gathering-of-the-suspects ploy that leads to a second fatality, but finally manages to see the light and solve the mystery.

The gilded cage of the title, in case you're wondering about it, is the name applied to the Cuban residence of the Henry Breeses.

Murder in the Gilded Cage is no towering edifice of brilliant detection, but it is a competent work from the typewriter of a possibly promising mystery writer who abandoned the form for what he thought was the more rewarding field of dramatic writing. (Charles Shibuk)

Wade Miller, *Guilty Bystander* (Signet, 1963; orig. 1947; 144 pp.)

Guilty Bystander is the second book by the Bob Wade/Bill Miller team, and the first of six featuring private eye Max Thursday. At the beginning Thursday is a down and out ex-private eye working as house detective in a shady hotel and drinking constantly. His ex-wife Georgia, now remarried, comes to him for help when their son Tommy is kidnapped. Max must sober up and use all his not inconsiderable skills to figure out the confusing scheme (which involves a million dollars worth of pearls) and rescue his son. As always in the Miller books the San Diego scene is vividly done, and Max is a sympathetic protagonist we want to succeed. Max gets some help from Homicide Lieutenant Austin Clapp (hero of Miller's first book, *Deadly Weapon*) and Smitty, an ex-madam who owns the hotel where Max works. It is a fine book that all hard-boiled fans will enjoy--Miller and Wade are excellent writers. (Jeff Meyerson)

Hake Talbot, *Rim of the Pit* (Bantom, 1965; orig. 1944; 170pp)

This book was chosen by Anthony Boucher for the World's Great Novels of Detection series, along with such classics as Christianna Brand's *Green for Danger* and Ellery Queen's *Cat of Many Tails*. Like those two this is an excellent book that should be far better known than it is (it was not mentioned by Barzun & Taylor). The detective is gambler Rogan Kincaid, who tries to determine a rational explanation for a couple of seemingly supernaturally caused murders.

Many years ago Grimaud Desanat froze to death in the North Woods. His wife Irene, a supposed medium, holds a seance to ask him about some trees he owned. During the seance Desanat appears and terrifies Irene, who is later found brutally murdered. The question is, who murdered her? Was it another member of the house party or the spirit of Desanat acting through another's body? More and more inexplicable events pile up that seem to favor the later theory, including a second murder that seems to clinch it, but Talbot makes it all come clear in a brilliant end. Talbot only wrote two detective novels, which may help to explain why he is so little known today, but *Rim of the Pit* is a classic of the genre that bears out Boucher's comparison with Carr and Rawson. (Jeff Meyerson)

Donald Hamilton, *Murderers' Row* (Fawcett, 1962; 144 pp.)

In *Murderers' Row*, Matt Helm's fifth case, things go wrong from start to finish. In order to find a scientist captured by the Russians, Mac wants a female agent to pretend to defect. When Helm is beating her up to make it look convincing, however, she suddenly dies. He refuses an order to come in for a "rest", and tries to complete the mission himself. He falls into a promising lead by luck through a meeting with Teddy Michaelis, the scientist's daughter. The finale comes on an eighty foot schooner in a raging storm in Chesapeake Bay. Though it's not one of his smoother jobs, Matt gets it done in the end. (Jeff Meyreson)

Erle Stanley Gardner, *The Case of the Queenly Contestant* (Morrow, 1967.)

Perry Mason's client this time around the track is a tall regal woman of about forty, who came to Hollywood twenty years ago after winning a beauty contest in the Midwestern town where she grew up. The hometown newspaper is about to run a "Whatever happened to . . . " story about the lady which for unstated reasons she is desperate to suppress. Mason soon learns that the big shot in his client's home town was recently lost at sea and that his will leaves a fortune to the illegitimate child he thinks he fathered twenty years before. The highspot of the book involves Mason bamboozling various sharpies into mistaking one of Paul Drake's female operatives for the queenly client. Everything else about the novel is hopelessly routine: the murder of a blackmailing nurse who knew the client's secret, the woman's arrest, the trial, all the customary scenes. Mason's "deductions" reach a new low in silliness and the courtroom plot twists are pure *Madame X*. Avoid at all costs. (Francis M. Nevins, Jr.)

Erle Stanley Gardner, *The Case of the Careless Cupid* (Morrow, 1968)

A well-kept widow, contemplating remarriage to a wealthy aging businessman, retains Mason to frustrate her beloved's greedy relatives who are trying to protect their expected shares of his estate by getting the widow convicted of poisoning her first husband. The subsequent legal maneuvers pack a good bit of the old Gardner drive and bounce, complete with excursions into offtrail subjects like taxidermy, the law of constructive trusts, and the conduct of lie detector tests. The plot is too simple, the trial perfunctory, the solution achieved by legwork concealed from the reader and presupposing some huge coincidences. (The murderer happened to choose the one type of weapon which would be useful when, months later, he decides to frme Mason's client.) But at least until the wrap-up, Gardner's rollercoaster for readers runs as swiftly as the fans expect. (Francis M. Nevins, Jr.)

Erle Stanley Gardner, *The Case of the Fabulous Fake* (Morrow, 1969.)
In the last Mason novel Gardner dictated before his death (the posthumously published Masons date from much earlier), the client is a young woman with a padded bra, a dying brother, an overnight case full of mysteriously acquired money and an absurd story. In the pre-murder bamboozlement sequence that had become as inevitable a feature of the Masons as the trial scene, Perry takes on a suave blackmailer who is threatening the young woman's future; but when the extortionist is shot and all the evidence points to Guess Who, Mason sheds his con man attire and becomes the courtroom wizard again. The plot is routine, the solution is rabbit-out-of-a-hat, but at least the story is unified and fairly intelligible, unlike a few other late Masons I could mention. (Francis M. Nevins, Jr.)

Robert Lee Hall, *Exit Sherlock Holmes* (Scribners, $7.95.)
It is a cliche that imitation is the sincerest form of flattery, and the pastiche is perhaps the sincerest of imitations. But the taking over and manipulation of another man's literary creations carries with it a considerable responsibility--a responsibility which, it must sadly be confessed, some recent writers of Sherlock Holmes pastiches have chosen to shirk.
Every person who has read and loved Arthur Conan Doyle's Sherlockian tales must surely regret there are only 56 short stories and four short "novels" in the canon. It is not unusual for even casual admirers of the Great Detective to read the entire Holmes saga several times during their lives, while the ardent Holmesian may actually lose count of the number of readings he has completed. Who would not, therefore, be delighted to learn that a new Sherlock Holmes story had been discovered? No one, surely, who had ever gone along with Holmes and Watson on one of their quests for the truth.
The brevity of the canon--the limited number of Holmes tales which Doyle ushered into print--and the understandable wish of the Holmes aficionado that there were more tales, account both for the recent boom in books and movies about Holmes and for the generally sympathetic reception these have received. If the taste is strongly enough acquired, the exhaust-on of the original sometimes results in the creation of the ersatz. It is never as satisfying, but it is better than nothing.
So long, that is, as the pastiche writer adheres substantially to the framework of the original. He may and must create new characters and plots, but the original characters must be treated with respect, as must their creator's intentions regarding them. If a would-be pastiche writer wishes to make substantial alterations in original characters--in their histories, their behavior, their personalities--he will best serve himself and his readers by creating entirely new characters of his own, and not trying to force borrowed characters into molds into which they do not fit.

This, unfortunately, is what Robert Lee Hall has done in *Exit Sherlock Holmes*. He has taken the familiar characters of Holmes, Watson, Mrs. Hudson, Lestrade, Gregson and Jones, and woven about them a tale in which Moriarty returns to bedevil Holmes and humanity, having miraculously survived his plunge into the abyss at Reichenbach falls. In order to rid the world of Moriarty once and for all, Holmes goes underground, not even telling the faithful Watson where he can be found. The bulk of the book recounts Watson's search for his friend, during which he encounters individuals from his and Holmes's past, and uncovers evidence which leads him to doubt that even he, who knows Holmes better than anyone else, really knows the Great Detective at all.

Hall handles the minor characters effectively, and his portrayal of Watson is intelligent, affectionate and convincing. It is with Holmes and Moriarty that *Exit Sherlock Holmes* becomes a travesty of the canon, which denigrates Holmes's greatness. To achieve his bizarre goal, Hall ignores or contradicts certain facts about Holmes which are given to us by Doyle, denies that a significant minor character in the saga ever existed at all, and--this is the greatest insult of all, both to Sir Arthur and to Sherlockians everywhere--asserts that two of the episodes of the saga are apocryphal.

Thus, in foisting this questionable pastiche upon the followers of Sherlock Holmes, Hall requires that we give up two of the 56 short stories entirely, and question the accuracy of most of the remainder. And for what? To accept a version of Sherlock Holmes of Hall's own creation which is neither so noble nor so deserving of respect and admiration as Doyle's original.

Though I, like other avid Holmesians, long for more accounts of the exploits of the world's first consulting detective, my longing is not so great that I will throw out the true gems in my possession to make room for this gaudy rhinestone. *Exit Sherlock Holmes* manages in a few cheap tricks to degrade the very character whom it purports to support. Which is a shame, for Hall clearly has skill as a writer and a grasp of the details of the Sherlockian world which could be turned to creating good and effective pastiches. But first he must learn to respect that which he would imitate. Until he does, his imitation will never flatter--it will only continue to insult. (Guy M. Townsend, reprinted from *The Memphis Commercial Appeal*, 15 May 1977.)

THE DOCUMENTS IN THE CASE
(LETTERS)

From Dorothy Juri, 175 Pineview Lane, Menlo Park, CA 94025: I am thoroughly enjoying my issues of *The Mystery Fancier*. I am new to this type of publication having found *The Armchair Detective* only one issue before its move to San Diego. /// On reading through part of your Wolfe Saga, I began wondering if anyone else beside myself remembers a movie long ago on Nero Wolfe. I don't remember who played Wolfe or what the picture was about but Archie Goodwin is and has always been Lionel Stander in my imagination. No matter how he is described I keep hearing that rasping voice and see Stander's face. /// Also on your comment about Dr. No, I seem to recall a plot used by Georgette Heyer in *Envious Casca* and Agatha Christie in *Murder at Christmas* or a title similar. /// You mention that women are in the majority in your subscribers, but I wonder how many of them like the slam bang detectives like Spillane etc. I am a "character & atmosphere" reader and dislike hard boiled detective writers. I have never read a Keeler or Brown and probably never will. /// As to the cost of your magazine, I think it is a good buy. When you indulge yourself in your enthusiasms, the cost has to be way out to outweigh your pleasure. /// Hope all the issues are as good as these first ones and I also hope it doesn't become a burden.
[*There were two Nero Wolfe movies, in both of which Archie was played by Lionel Stander. The first was the 1936* Meet Nero Wolfe, *based on* Fer-de-Lance, *and the second was* The League of Frightened Men *(1937). I have seen neither of them on the late movie circuit, but there appears to be a TV movie in the making, and there is talk of a TV series. Let's all hope . . . . /// I think you misread my comment about the proportion of men and women subscribers to* TMF: *the men are more numerous.*]

From Martha Sorrell, 302 W. Ohio St., Monticello, IN 47960: Your new format is very much O.K. Just means one thing to me, tho. I do not sit down and read it all at one time anymore. The print is too small. So I have to take my time reading it. Have always had the bad eyes so that is something I've learned to live with. /// By all means a checklist of the first 500 Pocket Books would be very interesting. The Pocket Books were one of the very first paperbacks published. At that time the price was 25¢. My, my that really dates me (ha). /// I have enjoyed your article on Nero Wolfe (The Nero Wolfe Saga). I am not a "dyed in the wool" Nero Wolfe fan but have read a good many of the books, novelets etc. at one time or another. As to your comment about the male subscribers outnumbering female subscribers 4 to 1 probably means that the males have more time on their hands to read your mag (ha). Do keep up the good work. I have enjoyed all five issues.

From Joe R. Lansdale, Rt. 2 Box 270-C, Nacogdoches, TX 75961: For the moment I'm not a subscriber, but through the kind-

ness of a friend I've read all your issues so far. . . . ///
I hope you don't mind an outsider and non-subscriber (at the
moment) butting in, but I did make some observations, and
like the preacher that's just returned from Christian Summer
Camp, I'd like to share them with you. /// First of all,
I'd like to say that I agree one-hundred percent with Jeff
Banks' statements about Pronzini's work. Bill's nameless
detective series is far superior to the work of Macdonald.
As a matter of fact, Macdonald's work strikes me as obviously "arty" and sicky sweet. Pronzini's detective may well be
the most believable of today's fictional private investigators. He's certainly one of the most interesting. /// I
was sorry to read that Avallone wasn't putting the readers
on. The whole thing seems pointless unless he was. It
would have been a good joke, but otherwise . . . . Well,
why not just print a blank sheet of paper? (Then again, you
wouldn't have gotten the feedback you got. Now would you?
In the words of Mrs. Littela, "Never mind.") /// Mike Nevins mentions William Colt McDonald's saddle sleuth Gregory
Quist. I'm not familiar with Quist, but there is an excellent series about a western detective named Jefferson Hewitt.
Hewitt is the brainchild of John Reese, a fairly prolific
western writer. To the best of my knowledge the books in
the series are *Weapon Heavy*, *Wes Harden's Gun*, *Texas Gold*,
and *The Sharpshooter*. Here again the man to see for an in
depth article is Jeff Banks. Jeff can add that to his list
of ten million and one things to do.

From Martin Wooster, Box 1691 Beloit College, Beloit, WI:
The Mystery Fancier 4 was as enjoyable as always, even if it
was the Incredible Shrinking Secret Decoder issue. Sorry to
hear you had problems with the Post Awful, but everyone
seems to have trouble with them sooner or later. I wish you
hadn't gone to as much trouble as you did; I would have gladly paid the 25¢ extra per issue if the poor reproduction and
shrunken type were the consequences of avoiding the Post Offal's surtax. Still, your zine is the only amateur press
publication I know that is delivered to the door four weeks
in *advance* of publication date--I admire you for it. (The
zine was postmarked 4 June and arrived on 6th June, if you
are worried about such things.) /// Barbato's piece on
mysteries and academia is interesting, but he's hopelessly
wrong about "Trevanian." The parents of a friend of mine
were long-time friends of Trevanian, so I can give more information on him than Barbato can. As I understand it, Trevanian was a senior bureaucrat in the Labor Department who
was afflicted with that disease that affects all (or nearly
all) mystery readers at one time or other--finishing a mystery and saying to oneself, "I can do better than this." So
he wrote *The Eiger Sanction* on nights and weekends. He had
not been to Switzerland before writing the novel and got all
his local color from books on mountaineering. After TES became a best seller, he quit the Labor Department and now
writes full-time. I am not prepared to reveal his real name,
but can say that his pseudonym was taken from his aunt, and
that he is at least part-Lebanese. (I'm not sure if he is
part-Canadian, as the setting of *The Main* would suggest.)
/// George Kelley may be interested to know that Koontz's

mysteries were the subject of controversy in the sf amateur magazine *Outworlds* about two years ago. The feud was started by Piers Anthony, and centered on what he considered inflated advances to Koontz of 70-100 thousand dollars per novel, and how the sf writer starves while the mystery writer stays in the lap of luxury. It degenerated into a cavalcade of raucous name-calling, but was fun while it lasted. /// The only problem with your Nero Wolfe series is that I'll have to read it twice--once in DAPA-Em, the second time in *TMF*. I wish you had revised it to take into account the criticisms made the first time around in DAPA-EM, but it's still fun reading, anyhow. I hope you revise the articles when you finish them and prepare the manuscript for publication. *The Nero Wolfe Companion*, perhaps? /// Marvin Lachman's suggestions for mystery reviewing are interesting, if a bit wrongheaded. He is correct when reviewing out-of-print material, but current material deserves more in-depth treatment. I could review the Mystery Library books in one paragraph or so, but that would not do justice to them. Thus the fuller treatment.

[*Poor reproduction! Compared to some amateur publications I have seen, TMF, even on lilac paper, is legibility incarnate. /// The Nero Wolfe Companion would be a very good title indeed. I'll keep it in mind--with your permission--when I start whipping the thing into shape for a book appearance (though I'll probably have to print it on my own mimeo). /// I'm inclined to the opinion that the older and less available books need longer and more detailed reviews, since many readers may never possess copies and the reviews may be all they ever see of them, while newer ones, being still widely available, can safely be treated with brevity.*]

From Jeffrey Meyerson, 50 1st Place, Brooklyn, NY 11231: It was quite a surprise to get the new issue so early, with the format being an even bigger surprise. I don't mind the smaller type (I have good eyesight), and I certainly don't mind getting *TMF* two or three weeks earlier. I do have a suggestion, however: if possible, could you use lighter colored paper, as the purple is tough to read? I thought the cover was sort of clever, actually. /// The articles were interesting as usual, though I wish Joseph Barbato identified "Trevanian." I'd like to see the Pocket Book checklist, if it's not too much of a chore for you. One of the advantages of being a DAPA-EM member is getting a head start on so many fine articles, not least of which is the Wolfe Saga. /// Martin Wooster is probably right about completeness in the Mystery Library reprints, but I don't see the point in judging them on the amount of new material. After arguing for completeness he turns around and suggests that the notes in *The Crooked Hinge* are familiar and should be dropped. He can't have it both ways. His review is a good example of the excessive detail that Marv Lachman is arguing against, though I think his suggestions go too far the other way. I prefer the middle ground: some idea of what the story's about without wholesale telling of plot. /// Even though I respect Mike Nevins' opinion, I still found *Nightmare in Pink* mechanical and contrived. No, I don't think *The Quick Red Fox* is "the high point of the whole series," not by a

long shot. /// Incidentally, another mystery writer in-joke
--in Bill Pronzini's latest, *Blowback*, one of the characters
mentions "Larry Ballard from the Kearny agency." Ballard is
one of the main characters in Joe Gores' DKA File Series;
last year Pronzini and Gores edited an anthology together.

From Bob Briney, 4 Forest Avenue, Salem, MA 01970:
Maintaining a regular bimonthly schedule for *TMF* means that
slowpokes like me have trouble keeping up. If I don't hurry,
I'll have three issues to comment on instead of two. /// The
most obvious point requiring comment is the new format. I
happen to like small print, but I'll bet you have other subscribers who don't share this peculiarity. Within reason,
any format which makes production easier and mailing cheaper
is OK. But I do hope you have not invested in a large stock
of that lavender-gray paper. . . . The fuzzier and fainter
printing produced by the electrostencilling would be bear-
able on light-colored paper, but a few pages of this gray-on-
gray is enough to turn me cross-eyed with strain. /// In
his letter in vln4, Mike Nevins mentions one pulp story by
John Dickson Carr. There is another--the only other story
that he wrote for the pulps, according to Carr himself.
This is "The Man Who Was Dead", which appeared in the May
1935 *Dime Mystery Magazine* under the byline John *Dixon* Carr.
Bill Clark called this story to my attention several years
ago. The misspelled middle name left the true authorship in
doubt, but I have just learned that Carr, in a letter to a
correspondent in 1970, conformed his responsibility for the
story. He blamed the misspelling on the magazine editor.
/// I'm glad to see your Nero Wolfe saga in *TMF*, though it
is slow reading--your comments keep tempting me to go back
and re-read the originals, and I'm not always able to resist.
Regarding "Bitter End", I assume you have seen the advertise-
ment in *Xenophile* #32 for *Corsage*, a limited edition collection of Rex Stout miscellany which includes this previously
unreprinted Wolfe story. (James A. Rock & Co., Publisher/
P.O. Box 1431/Bloomington, Indiana 47401; $6.50 for the pap-
erbound edition, or $13.50 for one of the 150 hardbound cop-
ies.) /// I enjoyed the reprint from *The Chronicle of Higher Education*. I wonder if Robert Parker's winning the MWA
Edgar for *Promised Land* is causing any alteration in his col-
leagues' reactions to his mystery writing career? /// Also
liked George Kelley's brief article on Dean R. Koontz. I
read the latter's *The Face of Fear* (as by "Brian Coffey") a
few weeks ago, and found it totally unconvincing. The idea
of the hero and heroine climbing down the outside of a building with mountain-climbing gear--ridiculous! /// That was
the night before George Willig made his ascent up the side
of the World Trade Tower . . . .
[*I used the "lavender-gray" paper (Gestetner labels it "lilac") for one reason only--it has less show-through than any
other mimeo paper I've ever seen. But you are quite right
about it being difficult to read from, and you will have
noted with relief that its use has been suspended. Actually,
the electrostencils I am using with this smaller format put
down much less ink than out stencils so show-through is not
such a problem now. In fact, I may even try to print this
issue on white paper, though I haven't yet decided. /// Yes,*

I saw the Xenophile *ad for* Corsage *(it was also advertised in AB Bookman's Weekly). The prices are outrageous and the failure to list any authors, editors or compilers is a rather peculiar, not to say suspicious, circumstance. I have a xerox copy of the original magazine appearance of "Bitter End," so I'm not going to rush out and buy a copy of* Corsage.]

From Robert M. Williams, Box 242, Rule, TX 79547:
The MYSTERY FANcier #4 is just as good as ever. I don't mind the new format. /// Somewhat hesitantly and also a little belatedly, I might add, I would like to mention a small matter concerning the Dell Checklist in *TMF* #2. The listings of #55 and #127 have the authors' names spelled wrongly. Instead of Peterson with an o, it should be Petersen with an e. This is a very common mistake made by most people. In fact, the cover of one of his books spells the name with an o, then corrects it inside. I never noticed myself until I began collecting his books, which, by the way, is an easy thing to do, as I know of only four he ever wrote. Petersen may be a woman, but somehow I can't conceive of a woman with even a nom de plume of Herman.

From George Kelley, 505 N. Carroll St., #503, Madison, WI:
Let me mention some obscure but very worthwhile articles I've run across. The first is in Gore Vidal's *Matters of Fact and Fiction: Essays 1973-1976* (Random, 1977). It contains a brilliant essay on the works of E. Howard Hunt. It's worth the price of the book (when it comes out in paperback). /// The second essay is in a book by Martin Green called *Transatlantic Patterns* (Basic Books, 1977). Green's book compares cultural patterns between the U.S. and England; the essay I want to recommend is "Our Detectives" which compares Sayers' Peter Wimsey with MacDonald's Travis McGee. Your local library should have it. /// Lately, I've been surprised at the books available in England and their quality of format. I'm speaking particularly of Richard Stark's Parker series (Coronet) and the fine James Hadley Chase series (Panther) with just beautiful covers. Help the Queen's economy by sending your order or request for catalogs to: J. Barnicoat (Falmouth) Ltd., P.O. Box 11, Falmouth, Cornwall TR 10 9EN, ENGLAND. /// In reading the James Hadley Chase books, I have an irresistable urge to ask Donald Westlake whether Chase's work influenced his writing of caper fiction, especially in the Parker series.
[*This is an excerpt from a letter to Steve Lewis. Steve sent it on to me and I don't think George will mind it being shared with TMF's readership.*]

From Peter Pross, 1303 Willis St., Richmond, VA 23224:
I enjoyed reading and rereading Volume One, Number Three. The book reviews submitted by Francis M. Nevins and Amnon Kabatchnik are especially enjoyable. Both reviewers offer more than a thumbnail sketch of plots and characters. /// Amen to Kabatchnik's closing remarks concerning *Croc', 'Gator* and *Alligator*. This is strictly conjecture, but I believe editor Townsend, after reading the reviews mentioned above, was inspired to ghost (tongue in craw) the review of

Beak! /// As a recent convert to collecting and reading
detective/mystery fiction, I would like to pose several questions to the readers of *The MYSTERY FANcier*. What do the
letters DAPA-EM denote? I realize they correspond to the
publication of the amateur mystery association. Still, and
despite repeated mention, I have yet to figure out what the
letters DAPA-EM stand for. /// Next, what is the basic purpose, intent and definition of a fanzine? Can *The Armchair
Detective* be classified as a fanzine? As an academic journal? As both? Or, none of the above? By coincidence last
month, my copies of *The Mystery Fancier* and *The Armchair Detective* both arrived on the same day. /// Also, are the
terms "detective/mystery fan" and "collector of detective
mystery fiction" synonymous? I would be interested in reading the responses elicited by these questions, which are offered to determine the perceptions of other collectors and
fans. /// Jeff Banks' letter contained several outstanding
suggestions--especially his thoughts concerning mystery
movie checklists. I don't know if I qualify for the title
of "certifiable nut," but I will attempt to periodically submit a mystery movie checklist. My first endeavor--a checklist of the mystery movies to which Raymond Chandler contributed, either as the novelist, screenwriter or scriptwriter--will be submitted next issue. Comments and suggestions from the readers of *The Mystery Fancier* would be most
helpful. /// My last remarks concern "The Nero Wolfe Saga:
Part One." There is no need to apologize for including your
installments into the pages of *The Mystery Fancier*. I believe "The Nero Wolfe Saga" will prove to be an informative
and interesting study of Stout's creation. You should, however, list the original publisher of each tale as well as
the place of publication. This would be a help to those of
us who are more bibliographically inclined. Also, on several occasions you indicate that an event or characteristic
may have appeared in an earlier tale but that you have neglected to mention it (i.e. Wolfe's lip routine, Wolfe's
practice of sending Archie from the room). I would suggest
that you strive to accurately "place" the first appearance
of such traits; uncertainty of this type, I'm afraid, detracts from "The Saga." /// Finally, I found several of
your comments about Archie's racism, Wolfe's sexism and
"Southern Belle phonies" superfluous and contradictory.
Statements of this nature ... "I take a rather forward position on the question of civil and human rights" (p. 18, *Too
Many Cooks*), and "There is nothing that makes my skin crawl
more than that sickening, affectatious Southern Belle Act"
(p. 27, "Cordially Invited to Meet Death") are strictly your
opinion. They are not relevant to The Saga of Nero Wolfe.
[*Later.*] Joseph Barbato's article as found in issue 4 of
The Mystery Fancier was one of the best articles to appear
to date. I might add that Professor Robin Winks has published a book entitled *The Historian as Detective* (I believe that is the correct title) which details the similarities between historians and detectives. /// One question,
what is the date and location of the 1977 Bouchercon?
[*When the first (and still the only) mystery amateur publication association was founded several years ago, the founder and first official editor, Donna Balopole, decided to*

christen it "Elementary, My Dear APA," the APA standing for amateur publication association. The acronym, had things rested there, would have been EMDAPA. Some editorial quirk--which, I understand, Donna has forgotten about by now--led her to transpose some of the letters, with the result that people are forever asking what the hell DAPA-EM stands for. Now you know (unless I've got it all wrong). Your other questions I will leave to TMF's readers to answer, with the request that they answer you through these pages rather than write directly to you. /// As for the Saga, let me explain once again how that series of articles came into being. The articles were begun with the sole intent of (hopefully) entertaining the fifteen-or-so members of DAPA-EM. DAPA-EM is a casual organization, and our individual magazines are in many ways like letters between friends. We take less care with what we write in them than we would, say, with something we might submit to TAD, and the interjection of personalities, biases, and the like are quite permissible, though there is not absolute agreement as to how large a part such tings should play in an apazine. So, the inclusion of my personal opinions in the original apazine articles was not, I think, out of place. As for my several references to items which I may have missed in earlier stories, I can only say that it wasn't until I had done half a dozen or so of the stories that I really decided to buckle down and do a thorough job on every tale, so I missed many items in the earlier stories. I will straighten everything out when I reread the stories again after I get through with the series. (I will also add complete bibliographical information at that time.) Now all this justifies the appearance of the Saga in my apazine, but different standards obtain for items published in a wider-circulation publication such as TMF, and here I can only plead that when I decided, for reasons already explained, to run the Saga in TMF I lacked both the time and the inclination to rewrite the articles for a different audience from which they were originally intended. I simply published them as they had appeared in my apazine, warts and all. [No, "Warts and All" is not the title of my apazine, though it wouldn't be a bad one at that.] However, there have been so many complaints about my personal comments that I will henceforth edit them out before printing the articles in TMF. Then maybe you folks will get off my back. /// Bouchercon 8 will be held in New York over the weekend of 7 October. For information send a SASE (#10 size) to Otto Penzler, 2771 Bainbridge Ave., Bronx, NY 10458.]

From Don Cole, 15355 Mason Plaza, Omaha, Nebraska 68154: I wasn't aware that TMF was in existence until Jeff Meyerson told me about it. It was then I immediately subscribed sight unseen. I have felt for many months that a great gap had been created when TMRN went under. I had even considered trying to organize something of my own to take its place. I am glad that you are on the scene and hope that you can hold out. TAD has its place in the field but in its new format is more like reading a course in college fiction than appealing to the interests of the amateur fan. As a past contributor to Mrs. Carlin's TMRN, I would be happy if time permits to help move things along. Although I am an ardent reader and collector of all phases of mystery fiction, my speciality is in "High Adventure Fiction," re, the Hammond Innes, Desmond Bagley, etc. A few years ago I wrote a rather lengthy article on High Adventure past and present in *TMRN*. The field has changed since then with the emergence of the popularity of Higgins and Bagley novels, so perhaps I could update it someday for you. /// I have read your first four issues of *TMF* and am appalled by the lack of cooperation among what must be a vast number of thriller nuts. It seems impossible that you are not getting a greater response. I can and have written several of my favorite authors and have received in return lengthy letters from them. Yet, in a periodical like yours, the same names appear weak after week and you have to rely so heavily on reviews. But hang tight and don't give up. In reading your comments, I realize you have the right temperament and wit to live through it all. I hate to be a downer but the new format just isn't the same as the first three issues. I'll bear with it and hope the other readers will, but the tabloid form is much more difficult to read. Where *TMF* can excel and pass *TAD* in some reader response is to leave the Sherlock Holmes, Agatha Christie, Ellery Queen critiques to *TAD* and concentrate on the many, many fantastic authors who are rarely mentioned. Surely most serious readers realize that the late Ed Lacy was one of the greatest "idea" men in the field. Although much of his work was through the paperback, and he was tremendously prolific, his standard of quality was amazing. Another great, late master was Fred Brown. What of the new breed writing with such a flair . . . Bill Pronzini, Robert B. Parker, Dennis Lynds writing as Mark Sadler and John Crowe, Arthur Lyons, Michael Z. Lewin, Joe L. Hensley, Colin Wilcox, Joe Gores, David Anthony, Duncan Kyle, Tony Hillerman, Warwick Downing, Alfred Harris and a host of others? What of old masters that wrote so well but were publicized so little and are still writing today . . . Bruno Fischer, Arthur Maling, Dan J. Marlowe, and the late Thomas Dewey. So much could be said about any of these authors. It seems to me that *TAD* spends a stupendous amount of time on mystery literature long past . . . all well and proper. But there is a great need for a *TMF* to tell us what's happening in the field today. Congratulations for your efforts and don't give up the ship.

www.ingramcontent.com/pod-product-compliance
Lightning Source LLC
Chambersburg PA
CBHW031428040426
42444CB00006B/731